T0198941

THOUGHTFUL INTELLIGENCE

A PRACTICAL GUIDE FOR MORAL DEVELOPMENT

MUSARRAT JABEEN Ph.D

authorHOUSE®

AuthorHouse™
1663 Liberty Drive
Bloomington, IN 47403
www.authorhouse.com
Phone: 1 (800) 839-8640

Published by AuthorHouse 10/15/2018

ISBN: 978-1-5462-6331-9 (sc)
ISBN: 978-1-5462-6329-6 (hc)
ISBN: 978-1-5462-6330-2 (e)

Library of Congress Control Number: 2018911925

Print information available on the last page.

Any people depicted in stock imagery provided by Getty Images are models, and such images are being used for illustrative purposes only. Certain stock imagery © Getty Images.

This book is printed on acid-free paper.

ACKNOWLEDGEMENTS

In the course of writing, 'Thoughtful Intelligence: A Practical Guide for Moral Development' I have incurred a considerable number of debts of warm gratitude. Indeed I am grateful to more people than I can recount. First of all I am grateful to 92 News HD Plus, Pakistan: watching 700 programs of 'Subh E Noor' televised by 92 news channel I am talented to write this book.

I appreciate my dependence on moral support of my mother Naseem Begum and father Attaullah to accomplish this book. I take pride in expressing my deep appreciation and gratitude to my mentors, Dr. A. A Qadeer Khan (Professor University of Karachi), Syed Salahuddin Ahmad (Professor University of Balochistan), and Tajammul Hussain (Advisor COMSATS).

I am grateful to have encouragement and guidance of my post doc supervisor Dr. Shumaila Yousafzai at Cardiff Business School UK.

My sincere thanks are due to the following prominent elite experts related to theme of my work, who in spite of their busy schedule, graciously granted knowledge to me: Nazir Ahmad Ghazi (Anchor Subh-e-Noor 92 News) Munir Ahmad Yousafi (Chief Editor Seedha Rasta Lahore), Tahir Hameed Tanoli (Assistant Director Iqbal Academy Pakistan), Brigadier ® Safdar Ali Shah (Director General CPEC), Dr. Muhammad Riaz (Former Director Quality Enhancement Cell NDU), Dr. Farrukh Saleem (Economist), Tahir Rasheed (LEAD Fellow), and a host of others.

Others who deserve my sincere thanks include my younger brother Mr. Muhammad Naveed and sister in law Dr. Rubeena Batool, my daughter Maria Jabeen Awwal, my son in law Muhammad Salman, my sons Muhammad Mustafa Awwal & Muhammad Sulaiman Awwal for appreciating my efforts to write this book.

I am grateful to Parvez Ahmad Butt (Former Secretary Science and Technology Government of Pakistan) for writing foreword and Humayun Javed (Student NDU) for writing prologue of this book. Lastly I must thank, Wazahat Rizvi, Aftab Mirza, Hadiqa Suhail, Rida Sajid and Yasir Afzal, who remained source of technical support to my studies.

FOREWORD

'Thoughtful Intelligence: A Practical Guide for Moral Development', is an incredible effort. I was literally thrilled to read it. The depth and detail are immense. It certainly can act as a beautiful manual for the moral development of individuals as well as societies. The collection and correlation of quotations with the text and analysis on a large number of the possibilities and impact of Thoughtful Intelligence is like a treasure.

Mr. Parvez Ahmad Butt,
Pioneer Executive Director,
Commission on Sciences and Technology for Sustainable Development in the South (COMSATS) and (Former Secretary Science and Technology Government of Pakistan), Islamabad.

PROLOGUE

'Thoughtful Intelligence: A Practical Guide for Moral Development,' addresses the most important struggle of our societies; the struggle to anchor from which the individual/collective actions need to be derived. The book is not just a conceptual masterpiece to motivate people to look beyond individualistic aspirations but also a practicable alternative to the contemporary pillars and practices on which the social environment stands.

"Thoughtful Intelligence" highlights the indispensable role of higher order thinking in decision making and observing the greater plot of life to find sustainability. The book is a must-read in the era of chaos. It serves as a beacon of light and a set of guiding principles for those who are eager for intellectual progress and common good rather than the fulfillment of materialistic and individualistic desires.

The book showcases the unique greatest mutuality composed of the Divine love, and care for human beings and the nature. Sharing this composition signifies the universality of thoughtful intelligence to familiarize the values of Affection, Tolerance, Patience, Generosity, Commitment, Appreciation of good, Condemnation of bad and contributing the best to humanity; for peace and prosperity. Rumi, Saadi, Ghazali, and Iqbal are found on the back of this work.

Dr. Musarrat Jabeen's effort to promote 'Thoughtful Intelligence' with pragmatic exercises deserves encouragement and appreciation of all of those who experience the book; in functional manner to practice, to communicate, and to participate in social strategy for moral development.

Humayun Javed
Student: BS/Spring, 2018
International Relations,
National Defence University, Islamabad

CONTENTS

Part II
Establishing Thoughtful Intelligence around you!

THOUGHTFUL INTELLIGENCE IS THE HIGHER ORDER OF THINKING

"By unrighteousness man prospers, gains what appears desirable, conquers enemies, but perishes at the root."

(Muhammad Iqbal, poet and thinker, 1877-1938)

Khizra[1] is righteous in prioritizing the upbringing of her three children for the best profit of the system of humanity. She believes that children are the only source of our immortality. She left her home town eight years ago because of security reasons and systemized her professional and family commitments as a single parent. Four years later she got an appointment in Islamabad. She could have kept the children in a smaller city where she was serving earlier by easily managing her lone being in Islamabad. But she was committed to provide her children with a quality guardianship; though they could have unique hostels and education in Abbottabad.

The challenge headed while finding a respectable residence in Islamabad. The space she got she had to earmark 25% of her salary. Even paying this much amount for the residence didn't match the needs of her three children; a separate room for each and a bit of space for the

---

[1] Khizra is a sustainable character in this book practicing the art of 'thoughtful intelligence' in her professional and family life. Her practices highlight her mutuality with the 'Creator', human beings and the nature.

helping hand. Furthermore, 35% of her salary went in education bill of the family. She decided to build her own residence after selling her house in another city of Pakistan. Her family has developed consensus to borrow only for education and health needs.

While constructing the house she chose a place after cognizance of water availability survey in Islamabad as per climate change predictions in future perspective. She consulted her children at each level and took them along to assess the places to give them the confidence of taking part in *decision making* and gathering experience to take *decisions* individually in their future.

Khizra and her children appreciate water and energy conservation. So while throwing ideas to build their home, they agreed to have buckets in the rest rooms instead of showers consuming excessive water. Each room has two windows to harvest sun to light and heat. The house favors the individuals with disabilities; wheel chair can move to basement and ground floor because of inbuilt ramps and wider doors of restrooms.

This day Khizra counts the results of her *thoughtful decisions*[2] regarding; work and family balance, fulfillment of housing requirement, health & education needs, and environment friendly habits in a family institution to enhance profitability in the system of humanity.

Khizra's mentor 'Qareeb,[3]' emphasizes that most precious is the one who realizes the impact of one's thought, word and action on others. Thoughtful intelligence renders the real power to manage all life affairs because:

- What we *think* we speak,
- What we speak we do,
- What we do frequently we practice,
- What we practice we communicate to others to do the same.

The conceptual basis of thoughtful decision making involves three abilities. It requires:

---

[2] Decision is a choice between alternative courses of action in a situation of uncertainty.
[3] Qareeb is the mentor of Khizra: who always guides her to realize the impact of her thoughts, words and actions on others' survival, dignity and development in time and space.

1) An ultimate sense of action and not of inefficient action
2) Super-relationship with human and natural resources
3) Awareness of future effects of decisions on others

It is a long term interest to foster thoughtful decision making. Thoughtful decision- making has distinction: as every decision is dynamic and put up with a thought process, while thoughtful decision making stands with the positive dynamics and thoughtfulness[4].

I was inspired to devise the concept of thoughtful intelligence[5] while teaching a course of 'Business Ethics: A Stakeholder and Issues Management Approach in 2010. A student asked me, "Who will determine what is wrong and what is right in our professional life?

I started to sieve my life when I heard the word righteousness (Achi baat in Urdu: Good notions in English) I was 4 years old. My mother used to take me to social gatherings and advised the following:

- Say Assalam-o-alaikum to everyone you encounter
- Say thanks when you are offered something
- Say sorry if you do something wrong to something belonging to somebody

These lines give the first potential to have connections with others to construct a righteous impression on others.

Then when my mother admitted me to school she advised the following:

- Say Asalam-o-alaikum to everyone you encounter; the fellows and teachers
- Follow the teacher's instructions
- Do your homework on time
- Keep your space clean in the class room

---

[4] Thoughtfulness is the capacity to understanding of what impact any word or act have on other person and refraining from it if one feels the impact will be negative; or making an effort to do it if the impact is to be positive.

[5] Intelligence is the thinking/learning capacity of an individual to process the information. Intelligence is the ability to assimilate the knowledge into practice.

These lines give the potential to have helpful connections with peers and teachers in a formal institution for better learning. Do keep in mind that my mother has no formal education.

I believe the above quoted *moral values* are synonymous in all the civilizations of humanity; they are righteous, they are universal and not debatable. They provide a thoughtful sensibility to *care for* others. Thoughtful intelligence is the foremost concept to initiate *righteousness.*

The more thoughtfully intelligent we are
The more righteous we are

Thoughtful intelligence has a significant relationship with *righteousness*. It is implied that different people take different decisions in a similar situation because of different level of thoughtful intelligence.

Thoughtful intelligence bases righteousness, and assents to care for human & natural resources and insinuates creative thinking to manage the present and future. Thoughtful intelligence consists of a specific capacity whereby the decision maker longs for sustainability of his/her decision, whether his/her leadership status continues or not.

Thoughtful intelligence is the higher order of thinking to train the mind-set to produce intentions and actions. Thoughtful intelligence can be struggled for and acquired. It is comprised of capacity to understand and realize the impact of one's thoughts, words and actions on others' (individuals', groups', and nations') survival, dignity[6] and development in time (days, weeks, months or years) and space (geographical land with or without human beings). It establishes thoughtful thoughts. Per the inner paradigm[7]: Thoughtful intelligence establishes and defends moral values in the individual against internal and external threats. This defense includes detection, prevention and response to threats through the use of moral beliefs, values, rules and practices. Thoughtful intelligence visions the eyes to observe and gives the courage[8] to

---

[6] Al-Quran, Bani Israel, Ayat: 70 'And We have certainly honored the children of Adam.'

[7] The inner paradigm is a framework containing all the accepted views of an individual about human life (past, present, and future); inclusive social, economic, political, and security dimensions.

[8] Courage is the ability to do something that frightens one: bravery.

understand befittingly suited to difficult times; and reveals compassion[9] for moral development.

The level of thoughtful intelligence drives the *morals* and prefixes all the concepts the skills of a personality because we express different personalities as follow:

1. The politician is a person of *Loyalty*; he takes national interest first and prefers the development of the nation instead of his own development.
2. The judge is a person of *Courage*; he stands firm in being a person of character and doing what is right, especially when it is unpopular or puts him at risk.
3. The professor is a person of *Humbleness*; he remembers that his ignorance is far greater than his knowledge.
4. The father is a person of *Integrity;* he tells the truth, exposes untruths, and keeps his promises.
5. The District Commissioner is a person of *Justice;* he stands for equally applied rules that respect the rights and dignity of all, and makes sure everyone obeys them.
6. The concerned citizen protects his mind and body as precious aspects of his *identity*; and extends same protection to every other person he encounters[10].
7. The teacher is a person of *responsibility*; he strives to know and do what is best, not what is most popular to build the character of the students.
8. The student is a person of *Self-Governance*; he has self-control, avoids extremes, and not gets influenced or controlled by others[11].

---

[9] Compassion is the ability to give and to forgive.

[10] Deborah. Norville, *The power of Respect: Benefit from the Most Forgotten Element of Success* (Edinburgh: Thomas Nelson, 2009), 43.

[11] "Defining Civic Virtue: Launching Heroes & Villains with your Students," accessed on Dec 16, 2016
http://billofrightsinstitute.org

The moral values: loyalty, courage, humbleness, integrity, Justice, respect, responsibility, and self-governance are the determinants mostly ignored to be imparted in prevalent education systems.

We must pause and think the moral systems[12] that connect us to all the human beings considered part of social, economic and political growth in the past, present and future. For example, honest business composes of all honest businessmen group in past in whichever civilization or country they were, they are or they would be. Now I take the leverage to present the conceptual model of this book project (See Table. 1).

Table 1. Deliberated concepts

Input Variables	Process Variables	Output Variables	Outcome Variables
Moral values	Mind-sets	Intentions & Actions	Impacts

Source: Self extract

Thoughtful intelligence heightens the operation of moral values because moral capital[13] enables the profitability of other forms of capital (See Table. 2). Zhao[14] interprets the concept, formation, and mechanism of the action of moral capital by illustrating the point that morality, as a spiritual element of capital or a kind of spiritual capital, clings to physical capital and affects the physical capital by playing a unique economic role. This book constructs a concept of moral capital nurtured by thoughtful intelligence connecting the seven types of capital.

---

[12] Moral system is a system of coherent and reasonable principles, rules, ideals, and values which works to form one's overall perspective of life. Not just any rules, of course, but moral values. Each one of you has a moral system you need to understand what a moral system is. Your moral system is your morality.

[13] Moral capital composes of moral concepts and practices of an individual.

[14] Xiaoxi. Wang, *On Moral Capital* (Bedford: MyWordShop, 2015), 55

Table 2: Tangible Types of Capital
Thoughtful intelligence arches 7 types of capital:

1. Thoughtful intelligence connects to the Natural Capital
2. Thoughtful intelligence connects to the Human Capital
3. Thoughtful intelligence connects to the Social Capital
4. Thoughtful intelligence connects to the Financial Capital
5. Thoughtful intelligence connects to the Manufactured Capital
6. Thoughtful intelligence connects to the Political Capital
7. Thoughtful intelligence connects to the Professional Capital

Source: Self extract

A thoughtfully intelligent person would instinctively operate the moral values but thoughtfully unintelligent person would not demonstrate commitment, courage or integrity in challenging situations. My 25 years of teaching and research experience in different universities reveals that people operate their mind-sets developed over the years before getting in the higher education. The experience intimated me to change myself first and then to facilitate the others to work as thoughtfully intelligent person.

By continuing to recognize and explore the causes of lack of moral development[15]; the effort is put into undoing the trend of meek moral development at all levels among the managers, faculty and students in higher education. As I began using these insights regarding thoughtful

---

[15] Moral development focuses on the emergence, change, and understanding of morality from infancy through adulthood. In the field of moral development, morality is defined as principles for how individuals ought to treat one another, with respect to justice, others' welfare, and rights. In order to investigate how individuals understand morality, it is essential to measure their beliefs, emotions, attitudes, and behaviors that contribute to moral understanding. The field of moral development studies the role of peers and parents in facilitating moral development, the role of conscience and values, socialization and cultural influences, empathy and altruism, and positive development. The interest in morality spans many disciplines (e.g., philosophy, economics, biology, and political science) and specializations within psychology (e.g., social, cognitive, and cultural). Moral developmental psychology research focuses on questions of origins and change in morality across the lifespan.

intelligence for moral development in my regular classes; parents of many students registered their appreciation for the behavioral change in their son/daughter studying at the university; that they could have never thought.

It inspirited my seven years of research to help develop and refine the insights about students, faculty and managers of higher education in this book. By learning in practical terms about how students and faculty are generally away from thoughtful intelligence, I realize that moral development needs to be struggled. With this awareness, this book may enlighten the mind-sets.

The application of thoughtful intelligence and understanding of moral development in the premises of globalization[16] is ultimate because of the kind and quality of thoughts being boosted over the young mind-sets leading to unlimited mental and material pursuits through high-tech media[17]. The scenario challenges the capacity of the youth to process the information available to respond because they are connected with the two societies; a society where they exist actually and the other where they are connected virtually.

To count the 65% bulk of youth in Pakistan it is necessary to create avenues of moral development in higher education. The result of conducting the seminars on 'Ethical Fitness'; I have been able to work on moral development programs with the application of thoughtful intelligence.

Opening the field of accommodation and increased conditioning with innovative trends to give and receive *facilitation*. I hope with

---

[16] Globalization processed by fast communication has transmitted thoughtless language and practices, promoted individualism, and consumerism that badly impacted the institution of family.

[17] Junk Food for the Mindset, "When asked what one did over the weekend, we often hear the boast, 'Oh, I binge-watched Game of Thrones' or one of the other numerous series of cluttering the airwaves. Coupled with other online distractions like play stations and social media, the opportunity for healthy mental pursuits is almost non-existent. Since we do not study history and literature or study science and technology, our mental faculties are not being developed to their potential. As a result, we can't debate with any sense of authority, nor can we see beyond the surface of an issue. Our reactions are usually knee-jerk as we lack any background knowledge of national or world affairs. Make sure you are staying away from 'junk food for the mind' and are following a healthy reading 'exercise' plan with lots of mind games thrown in. Junk food leads to diabetes and obesity, junk food for the mindset can be worse." Accessed Nov 13 2017, **http//:www.DAWN.com**

this awareness the practitioners will go beyond the suggestions in this book and continue to develop ways in which you can relate to moral development.

Thoughtful intelligence reveals new strategies for moral development by first recognizing training of the mind-set. It then offers practical suggestions about how one can get rid of frustration and inside waste and then to fill in with thoughtful resolutions. Moral development does not have to be such a struggle; only when we lack the capacity to understand and realize the impact of our thoughts, words and actions on others' (individuals', groups', and nations') survival, dignity and development.

Many people are frustrated because they live but do not know how to make things better for themselves and for others. Through understanding how context, paradigm and practices are different in this Wi-Fi age you will learn new ways for successfully relating with, listening to, and managing the opposing notions. You will learn how to create the moral development you deserve.

The expansion of thoughtfully intelligent individuals helps to locate healthy forces for moral development. Impediments in the way of moral development can be dissipated or avoided. When you realize that you have to change yourself and to facilitate the other to change, you can cooperate for change.

Most important, throughout this book you will learn practical techniques for creating *caring* relationships. Many examples will simply and concisely express what you have always intuitively known. This validation will assist you in being you and in not losing yourself in your moral development.

It is inspirational to compile the treasured values of thoughtful intelligence for moral development in a manual form. The results of this program for understanding moral development are immediate as well as lasting. Certainly the journey of creating moral development can be rocky at times. Problems are inevitable. But these problems either can be sources of threat or can be opportunities for deepening intimacy and increasing care, and trust in you and around you.

I have made specifications about thoughtful and thoughtless individuals in this book. If this is the case, then by applying the suggestions, strategies, and techniques in this book you not only will create more passion in your relationships but also will increasingly balance your complex characteristics.

In this book I do not directly address the question of why moral development has been let down in higher education. This is a complex question to which there are many answers, ranging from parental influence, education and cultural conditioning by society, the media and history are available. The benefits of applying the insights in this book are immediate.

In the consistent predicament of moral depravation we need a positive picture to locate the healthy forces for moral development *in and around us.* This book provides that vision. Even if our past was better, times have changed, and a new approach to re-approach relationship for moral development is required. It is essential to think and practice morals. I believe everyone can benefit from the insights of this book.

It is never too late to increase the morality in your life. You only need to learn a new way. If you need *contentment*, this book is for you.

It is a pleasure to share Thoughtful Intelligence with you. After all, our children do deserve a better world.

Invent your thoughtful version after reading this book. All books talk, but this book tries to listen as well. BECOME A THOUGHT LEADER!

Thoughtful intelligence is a practical guide for moral development in the 21st century. It reveals how moral development relates to all areas of life. Not only moral development icons itself rather it benevolent the social, economic and political development. A thoughtfully intelligent individual thinks, feels, perceives, reacts, responds, and appreciates differently.

Moral: Thoughtfully intelligent individuals are the signs of sustainability of humanity.

Exercise

Try this book.

Please rise to say:

May we are blessed to have the help for the righteous path for human survival, dignity and development.

CHAPTER 1

THOUGHTFUL INTELLIGENCE IS DYNAMIC APPLICATION TO TRAIN THE MIND-SET

Prophet Muhammad (PBUH) says:

> »إنَّمَا الْأَعْمَالُ بِالنِّيَّاتِ «
>
> **"Indeed there is relationship between intentions and actions[1]."**

Khizra was writing her M. Phil thesis in 1998 with a sub focus on child labor. Hussain a boy of nine years was introduced to her to help in household chores because she had to care for her daughter born in 1997 and a son born in 1998. In one view, it was of course child labor; Khizra should not have chosen Hussain to serve.

At once she got hooked another thought. The parents of Hussain were not able to pay for his education. Khizra was unable to offer him free education and space. Hussain desired both as he was from the countryside. Khizra was in great need of a helping hand. She chose Hussain to manage the cleaning and clothes in the morning, so she could study. In the evening Hussain was able to attend school. He passed grade 5 (primary school education) and qualified middle school education as well. He was called Hussain Bhai by the children; his meal plate was always equal to the children's meal plate. Khizra always ensured that he

---

[1] "Islamic center for research and academics," accessed March 5, 2018 http://icraa.org/hadith

1

got eight hours of sleep daily. He was offered a monthly salary that his parents could prosper. He enjoyed T. V entertainment with the children. He became Quran and computer literate. He also got the opportunity in Abbottabad to learn Karate with Khizra's children, once her husband was posted there. He earned a 'green belt' (a level in karate). Khizra's mother taught Hussain the skills to produce jams and pickles. He became a very good cook. Later on, he learned how to tailor gents' clothes. With all this he was encouraged to learn the skills of automobiles repairs. In 2010 after fourteen years of service to Khiza, he was able to earn 25000 rupees per month, equaling the salary of a research assistant in any public sector university of Pakistan. Hussain had an excellent sense of *honesty, loyalty, cleanliness, sobriety, piety, and patience.* Khizra believes that her children's growth with Hussain was a blessing from 1997 to 2010.

This day, Khizra counts the results of her *thoughtful intelligence to train the mind-set[2]* regarding social issue of child labor and its practical management, the fulfillment of Hussain's, Khizra's and her children's education and moral training in a family institution to enhance profitability in the system of humanity.

Khizra's mentor Qareeb pronounces that the thoughtful mind-set has more power than hands: hands grasp the material, but the mind-set changes it.

In chapter 1 you will study the following concepts of thoughtful intelligence.

    I. Relatives of thoughtful intelligence
    II. Essentials of thoughtful intelligence
    III. Supremacy of morals
    IV. Thoughtful intelligence works

"Every civilization depends upon the quality of individuals it produces".
Frank Herbert (American fiction writer, 1920-86)

---

[2] A mindset is described as the mental inertia of an individual. It is a set of ideas, beliefs, values, rules and practices used as the bases for making judgments and decisions. Mindset is a mental attitude that benchmarks an individual's intentions, words, and actions that impact the growth, expansion and success.

Thoughtfulness is the capacity to show understanding of what impact any act or word has on other persons and refraining from it if one feels the impact will be negative. This also includes of making an effort to do it if the impact is to be positive[3].

Human intelligence has been defined as one's capacity for logic, understanding, self awareness, learning, planning, creativity, and problem solving. It can be more generally described as the ability or inclination to perceive or deduce information, and to train it as knowledge to be applied towards adaptive behaviors within an environment or a context. "Intelligence is the whole of cognitive or intellectual abilities required to obtain knowledge, and to use that knowledge in a good way to solve problems that have a well described goal and structure.[4]" Kutz[5] opined that intelligence is the ability comprised of brainpower and aptitude to comprehend; and profit from thinking. Intelligence delineates the thinking/learning capacity of an individual. Intelligence is the ability to assimilate the knowledge into practice.

Thoughtful intelligence is the higher order of thinking to train the mind-set to produce intentions and actions. Thoughtful intelligence can be struggled for and acquired. It is comprised of capacity to understand and realize the impact of one's thoughts, words and actions on others' (individuals', groups', and nations') survival, dignity[6] and development in time (days, weeks, months or years) and space (geographical land with or without human beings). It establishes thoughtful thoughts. Per the inner paradigm[7]: Thoughtful intelligence establishes and defends moral values in the individual against internal and external threats. This defense includes detection, prevention and response to threats through the use of moral beliefs, values, rules and practices. Thoughtful

---

[3] Zubeida Mustafa is a Journalist who worked for DAWN from 1975 to 2008 and now writes a weekly column for Daily DAWN), Pakistan.

[4] Nicholas. Mackintosh, *IQ and Human Intelligence* (UK: Oxford University Press, 2011), 55.

[5] Matthew R. Kutz, "Toward a Conceptual Model of Contextual Intelligence: A Transferable Leadership Construct" *Leadership Review*, Vol. 8 (Winter 2008): 18-31.

[6] See Alquran, Sura Bani Israel, Ayat:70 'And We have certainly honored the children of Adam'

[7] The inner paradigm is a framework containing all the accepted views of an individual about human life (past, present, and future); inclusive social, economic, political, and security dimensions.

intelligence visions the eyes to observe and gives the courage[8] to understand befittingly suited to difficult times; and reveals compassion[9] for moral development.

The individual is socially constructed. He or She expresses demand and supply of moral values in regulating and disposing of behavior in personal and public paradigms. Its acquisition and application becomes complex as it is tied to the below eleven questions. The individual's mind-set training has a collective aspect as well because it contributes to collective construction of the society. The collective aspect enables the community as a whole to benefit from individual construction. There must be an appropriate balance between the individual and collective aspects.

1. What is the relationship of the individual to the concepts of time and space?
2. What are the *moral values[10]* of the individual?
3. What are the *internal* threats[11] to the moral values of the individual?
4. What are the *external* threats[12] to the moral values of the individual?
5. How does the individual thinks and practices the relationship to the past, present and future?
6. How does the individual thinks and practices the relationship to the *natural environment[13]*?
7. How does the individual thinks and practices the relationship to the *social environment[14]*?

---

[8] Courage is the ability to do something that frightens one: bravery.
[9] Compassion is the ability to give and forgive.
[10] Moral values include: humbleness, love, kindness and modesty.
[11] Internal threats include: arrogance, anger, vengefulness and lust in-side the individual.
[12] External threats: arrogance, anger, vengefulness and lust in-others around the individual.
[13] The natural *environment* encompasses the interaction of all living species, climate, weather, and *natural* resources that affect human survival and economic activity.
[14] The *social environment includes* the immediate physical and *social* setting in which individual lives with certain developments. It includes the material and non material culture that the individual is educated.

8. How does the individual thinks and practices the relationship to the *economic environment[15]*?
9. How does the individual thinks and practices the relationship to the *political environment[16]*?
10. How does the individual thinks and practices the relationship to the *judicial behavioral environment[17]*?
11. How does the individual thinks and practices the relationship to the *community, province, and state he or she belongs*?

Exercise

How many of the above questions do you realize in your being?

I. Relatives of thoughtful intelligence

Studying thoughtful intelligence means establishing individual potential in the production of moral development. There is hardly any work on thoughtful intelligence. But the study may utilize the contiguous literature regarding, social intelligence, multiple intelligence, emotional intelligence, moral intelligence and ethical intelligence.

In 1920, for instance, E.L. Thorndike[18] described *"social intelligence"* as the skill of understanding and managing others.

In 1983 Gardner[19] introduced his theory of *"multiple intelligence"* in his book, *'Frames of Mind'*, which is known as systematic, multidisciplinary and scientific depicted from psychology, biology,

---

[15] The economic environment includes the totality of *economic* factors, such as employment, income, inflation, interest rates, productivity, and wealth that influence the politico-economic institutions and the buying behavior of consumers.

[16] The *political environment* includes government and its institutions and legislations and the public and private stakeholders who operate and interact with or influence the social, economic and decision making systems of the state.

[17] The *Judicial behavioral environment* is best understood as a function of the incentives and constraints that legal systems place on their judges in certain communities or states to impart justice to the individuals.

[18] R.L. Thorndike, "Factor analysis of social and abstract intelligence." *Journal of Educational Psychology*, 231-233. (1986): 27

[19] H.Gardner, *Frames of mind: The theory of multiple intelligences* (New York: Basic Books, 1983).

sociology and the arts & humanities. According to Gardner[20], intelligence is much more than IQ because a high IQ in the absence of productivity does not equate to intelligence. In this description, "Intelligence is a bio-psychological potential to process information that can be activated in a cultural setting to solve problems or create products that are of value in a culture[21]." Gardner also favors gathering ethnographic data and cross-cultural information to see intelligence in action and in context. Following this description it can be assumed that the decision makers try to perform in regards to their distinctive capacity and situation. "Monopoly of those who believe in a single general intelligence has come to an end[22]." He emphasized that there are at least seven ways ("intelligences") that people understand and perceive the world. Gardner lists the following:

- Linguistic: the ability to use spoken or written words.
- Logical-mathematical: inductive and deductive thinking and reasoning abilities (logic, as well as the use of numbers)
- Visual-spatial: the ability to mentally visualize objects and spatial dimensions.
- Body-kinesthetic: the wisdom of the body and the ability to control physical motion.
- Musical-rhythmic: the ability to master music as well as rhythms, tones and beats.
- Interpersonal: the ability to communicate effectively with other people and to develop relationships.
- Intrapersonal: the ability to understand one's own emotions, motivations, inner states of being, and self-reflection.

The verbal-linguistic and logical-mathematical intelligences are the ones most frequently used in traditional school curricula. A more balanced curriculum that incorporates the arts, self-awareness, communication, and physical education may be useful to leverage the intelligences that some students may have.

---

[20] H. Gardner, *Intelligence reframed: Multiple intelligences for the 21ˢᵗ century* (New York: Basic Books, 1999).
[21] Ibid
[22] Gardner (1999) Op cit

Historical data and historical records are readily available to assist in many decision problems, the application of this information is called *cumulative intelligence*. Often historical data is incorrectly managed and due to over complication of their weighting and application in a decision making process is ignored. The management and effective use of cumulative intelligence in the decision making process is critical.

Daniel Goleman's model focuses on '*Emotional Intelligence*' as a wide array of competencies and skills that drive leadership performance. It consists of the following five areas:

- Self-awareness: one knows one's emotions, strengths, weaknesses, drives, values and goals and recognizes one's impact on others while using gut feelings to guide decisions.
- Self-regulation: manages or redirects one's disruptive emotions and impulses and adapts to changing circumstances.
- Social skills: one manages others' emotions to move people in the desired direction.
- Empathy: one recognizes, understands, and considers other people's feelings especially when making decisions
- Motivation: one motivates oneself to achieve for the sake of achievement.

To Golman, emotional competencies are not innate talents, but learned capabilities that must be worked on and can be developed to achieve outstanding performance. Goleman believes that individuals are born with a general emotional intelligence that determines their potential for learning emotional competencies[23]. Goleman's model of EI, has been criticized in the research literature as being merely "pop psychology." However, EI is still considered by many to be a useful framework especially for businesses.

Bruce Weinstein[24] premises that '*Ethical intelligence*' indeed creates the most fulfilling life. Weinstein lists principles of ethical intelligence as follows:

---

[23] Daniel, Goleman. *Emotional Intelligence: Why It Can Matter More Than IQ.* (New York: Bantam Books, 2005).

[24] Weinstein, B. *Ethical Intelligence: Five Principles for Untangling Your Toughest Problems at Work and Beyond.* (California: New World Library, 2011).

- Do no harm: harm is from minor harm to death. Prevent harm and minimize preventable harm.
- Make things better: flight attendant tells us, 'should the cabin lose pressure, oxygen masks will drop down from the overhead area. Please put one over your own mouth before you attempt to help others.' Why? Because the only way we can hope to be of service to others is we are in good shape ourselves.
- Respect others: ethically intelligent people show respect in the deeper sense by honoring the values, preferences, and most important, the rights of others.
- Be fair: fairness is about giving others their due resources.
- Be-loving: It seems hard to fathom in a business context, just think of care, for example petty gestures at work.

In fact, all five principles mentioned above provide the guidelines for making the best possible decisions in every area of life. These principles have legal, financial and psychological implications; and they are the core of ethical intelligence.

II. Essentials of thoughtful intelligence

The essentials of thoughtful intelligence are as follow:

1. Observation: observing self for self assessment.
2. Cleansing inside: (Greater Jihad).
3. Recognition: of relationship with human and natural resources.
4. Realization: of future effects of decisions in time and space.
5. Moral clarity: by an articulate human conception of moral justice.
6. Action: An ultimate sense of action and not of inefficient action
7. Righteousness: Thinking and comprehending that where the actions are counted; in the list of good deeds or bad deeds.

III. Supremacy of morals

Ethics are generally *accepted* moral principles; whereas morals are universally *appreciated* principles of righteousness. Values are described as individual or personal standards of what is valuable or important to an individual.

Moral values are those preferences that are integral to the moral reasoning process. A moral decision is a choice made based on an individual's ethics, manners, character and what he believes is righteous behavior. Moral reasoning is the mental process that is set in motion to come to some decision of right or wrong in any moral dilemma.

Morals are universal in time and space: They have been appreciated in the past, are appreciated at present and it is assumed that they will be appreciated in future as well. In fact, morals may be defined as the conduct that reflects universal principles essential to leading a worthwhile life and for effective self-governance. For many leading founders of the nation state system, attributes of character such as justice, responsibility, perseverance, and others were thought to flow from an understanding of the rights and obligations of men[25].

'Moral intelligence' is the capacity to understand right from wrong and to behave based on the value that is believed to be right. Moral intelligence was first developed as a concept in 2005 by Doug Lennick and Fred Kiel[26]. Most of the research involved with moral intelligence agrees that this characteristic is ability-based. Therefore, moral intelligence is seen as a skill that can be further developed with practice. Moral intelligence is the central intelligence for all humans. Moral intelligence is distinct from emotional and cognitive intelligence[27].

There are two models of moral intelligence one was presented by Doug Lennick and Fred Kiel, authors of *Moral Intelligence* and the originators of the term. Both of them identified four competencies of moral intelligence in their models: integrity, responsibility, forgiveness, and compassion. The other model of moral intelligence was proposed by Michele Borba in her book *'Building Moral Intelligence: The Seven Essential Virtues that Teach Kids to Do the Right Thing'*. Borba registered seven essential virtues of moral intelligence: empathy,

---

[25] "Defining Civic Virtue: Launching Heroes & Villains with your Students," accessed on Dec 16, 2016,
http://billofrightsinstitute.org
[26] M. Borba, *Building Moral Intelligence: The Seven Essential Virtues that Teach Kids to Do the Right Thing.* (San Francisco: Jossey-Bass, 2002).
[27] Ibid

conscience, self-control, respect, kindness, tolerance, and fairness. She gives a step-by-step plan for parents to teach their children these virtues in order to enhance their moral intelligence.

In shades of above content I move on *thoughtful intelligence (*see Table 1.1*)*. It pertains to beliefs, values, rules and practices in past-present-future vis-à-vis moral capacity of an individual. Thoughtfulness has significant relationship with righteousness. It has been implied that different people take different decisions in a similar situation because of different levels of thoughtfulness. Thoughtful intelligence based on righteousness, assents to care for human & natural resources and norms of creative thinking to manage the present and future.

Table: 1.1 Thoughtful intelligence

Thoughtful intelligence is the higher order of thinking to train the mind-set to produce intentions and actions. Thoughtful intelligence can be struggled for and acquired. It is comprised of capacity to understand and realize the impact of one's thoughts, words and actions on others' (individuals', groups', and nations') survival, dignity[28] and development in time (days, weeks, months or years) and space (geographical land with or without human beings). It establishes thoughtful thoughts. Per the inner paradigm[29]: Thoughtful intelligence establishes and defends moral values in the individual against internal and external threats. This defense includes detection, prevention and response to threats through the use of moral beliefs, values, rules and practices. Thoughtful intelligence visions the eyes to observe and gives the courage[30] to understand befittingly suited to difficult times; and reveals compassion[31] for moral development.

---

[28] Al-Quran, Sura Bani Israel, Ayat: 70 'And We have certainly honored the children of Adam.'

[29] The inner paradigm is a framework containing all the accepted views of an individual about human life (past, present, and future); inclusive social, economic, political, and security dimensions.

[30] Courage is the ability to do something that frightens one: bravery.

[31] Compassion is the ability to give and to forgive.

IV. Thoughtful intelligence works

Thoughtful intelligence bases the shared value[32] of profit for the system of humanity, as this value is revealed and appreciated over time and space in all the human civilizations. It thoroughly benchmarks and fares contentment; it works with sorrow and happiness for a change by utilizing connectivity between the creator and His creations. Respect of human beings means humanity[33].

Iqbal says:

> آدمیت احترام آدمی با خبر شو از مقام آدمی
>
> Humanity means respect of the mankind-
> learn to appreciate the true worth of man.

Thoughtful intelligence *builds thinking habits* that impact mental, emotional and physical states of the individual.

Thoughtfulness consists of specific capacity whereby the decision-maker longs for *sustainability of his/her decision* in time and space, whether his/her leadership status continues or not.

Thoughtful intelligence *evolves the thoughts* in the individual that eliminates everything extra to profitability to the system of humanity through inside cleansing.

Thoughtful intelligence *expands the human sensors* so that the individual becomes sensitive about others and flourishes in the greater sense of belonging.

Thoughtful intelligence is *aspired by wisdom*, supported by knowledge, uttered by tongue and displayed through practice.

---

[32] Value of profit for the system of humanity is holistic, universal and sustainable.

[33] The quality of being human is comprised of two qualities:
Benevolence: compassion, brotherly love, fellow feeling, humanness, kindness, kindheartedness, consideration, understanding, sympathy, tolerance, goodness, good-heartedness, gentleness, leniency.
Mercy: mercifulness, pity, tenderness, benevolence, charity, generosity, magnanimity.

Thoughtful intelligence *insinuates the sense of environmental sustainability.* It reminds the "7ᵗʰ generation" principle taught by Native Americans: that in every decision, be it personal, governmental or corporate, we must consider how it will affect our descendents seven generations into the future; so that the pristine sky, field and mountains in this photo will still be here for them to enjoy. Thoughtful intelligence offers capacity of decision making, inquiring and *learning.*

Thoughtful intelligence grac*es a variety of cloaks*[34] (See Table. 1.2) fit into all scenarios of righteousness vs wrong, sorrow vs happiness, and good vs evil.

Table 1.2 Thoughtful intelligence and the variety of cloaks	
1.	*Cloak* of *Patience*
2.	*Cloak* of *Generosity*
3.	*Cloak* of *Commitment*
4.	*Cloak* of *Appreciation*
5.	*Cloak* of *Hospitality*
6.	*Cloak* of *Confession*
7.	*Cloak* of *Covering the others faults*
8.	*Cloak* of *Condemnation*
9.	*Cloak* of *Contributing the best to humanity*

*What the individual would like to wear and when to wear?
Source: Self extract

---

[34] A loose outer garment, as a cape or coat that covers body or mindset for example, "He conducts his wealth under a *cloak* of generosity."

Exercise

Count, how many cloaks you have as your belonging.

Thoughtful intelligence *empowers* because realization of the greater being and connections; makes an individual prismatic. *Thoughtful intelligence facilitates to acquire 'Khudi'as per the concept of 'Self'given by Allama Iqbal.*

Contentment is always evolved through the practices of chastity, piety, love and compassion. It happens when the individual wears the cloaks of appreciation, generosity, forgiveness, patience, hospitality, philanthropy and confession.

Chapter 2 offers standard operating methods to acquire thoughtful intelligence.

Chapter 3 of this book deliberates the (Tazkia Nafs------Inside Cleansing) inside cleansing of the individual's physical and metaphysical mechanisms. It erects the purity of self-submission to the system of humanity.

Chapter 4 offers thought resolutions for the cleaned mind-set.

Chapter 5 highlights mutuality with nature and human beings as a source of change.

Chapter 6 deliberates informal moral development while chapter 7 strategizes formal moral development.

Moral: Being thoughtless is the real threat to mankind's livability[35] on earth!

Exercise

Reserve the best quality of yours' to make the world livable for others.

Please rise to say:

May we are able to grow in thoughtful intelligence beyond material way of life.

---

[35] **Livability** is the sum of the factors that add up to a community›s quality of life—including the built and natural environments, economic prosperity, social stability and equity, educational opportunity, and cultural, entertainment and recreation possibilities.

CHAPTER 2

STANDARD OPERATING METHODS TO ACQUIRE THOUGHTFUL INTELLIGENCE

Khizra became the head of the department at university in 2008. At the time of result announcement, Hidayatullah (a student) moved fervently in her office to complain that he was marked zero in the research report column. The matter was investigated and found that he submitted the research report but his report was left unattended mistakenly (by the staff) in the cupboard. This grave negligence could have cost Hidayatullah another term at the university.

Khizra went all alone to contest his case with the higher authorities. The inquiry committee was established, and the case was interrogated several times to ensure the *procedural justice*. Finally, Hidayatullah's research report was sent for examination and marked with significance. The entire process took four months. Khizra had to rush from office to office to get things positive in all dispositive trends. That day Khizra counted that the leader has to *take the responsibility* for any mistake that arises in the system and has to correct it thoughtfully for modeling righteousness.

Khizra's mentor Qareeb advises, "We must count on what goes on around us as we weave our path in life, to adjust our direction and goals as necessary to fit the environment we are operating within."

Thoughtful intelligence is the higher order of thinking to train the minds-et to produce intentions and actions. Thoughtful intelligence can be struggled for and acquired. It is comprised of capacity to understand

and realize the impact of one's thoughts, words and actions on others' (individuals', groups', and nations') survival, dignity[1] and development in time (days, weeks, months or years) and space (geographical land with or without human beings). It establishes thoughtful thoughts. Per the inner paradigm[2]: Thoughtful intelligence establishes and defends moral values in the individual against internal and external threats. This defense includes detection, prevention and response to threats through the use of moral beliefs, values, rules and practices. Thoughtful intelligence visions the eyes to observe and gives the courage[3] to understand befittingly suited to difficult times; and reveals compassion[4] for moral development.

To secure thoughtful intelligence following standard operating methods can be realized:

    I. Context to acquire thoughtful intelligence
    II. Vision of thoughtful individual
    III. Self Assessment for thoughtful change
    IV. Required Individual competencies for thoughtful change
    V. Required systematic competencies for thoughtful change
    VI. Automation of thoughtful change

I. Context to acquire thoughtful intelligence

The context to acquire thoughtful intelligence reels on realization of purpose of life and realization of gain and loss.

Realization of the Purpose of life: The purpose of life must be identified keeping in view the connectivity to creator, and creatures. We must touch upon the most important and the central theme of Rumi's philosophy and poetry which the world needs now more than ever before; the quest for Divine Love. It is the love for fellow human beings,

---

[1] Al-Quran, Bani Israel, Ayat: 70 'And We have certainly honored the children of Adam.'
[2] The inner paradigm is a framework containing all the accepted views of an individual about human life (past, present, and future); inclusive social, economic, political, and security dimensions.
[3] Courage is the ability to do something that frightens one: bravery.
[4] Compassion is the ability to give and to forgive.

without regard to color, race or religion. That leads ultimately to path of the Divine Love[5]. The following *Seven* principles will help.

1. Realize life is a gift and a profound responsibility: demonstrate genuine sense of appreciation for the privilege of family, community and nation, and an authentic sense of personal responsibility to positively affect your family, community and nation.
2. Reinvent yourself: demonstrate the ability to try new approaches to solve life problems. Acknowledge that the approach being taken is not working. Change your way of thinking and interacting with family, and companions.
3. Teaching and mentoring: take time to teach and mentor, and to be taught and mentored.
4. Making difficult decisions: take the ownership of problems and challenges and make tough decisions. Mobilize the people around to consider the best approaches and communicate the rationale for decisions that are made and provide information as to the outcomes and effectiveness of the decision.
5. Set a great example: make the appearance in the situation by modeling righteousness.
6. Cultivate talent: provide appropriate support to people around you in family and profession to be successful in new endeavors.
7. Care about the right things: the words and actions should communicate and preach about the righteousness.

The performance of intentions and actions must be organized on the bases of appropriation to situation in future terms interlocking the existing ones. Individual mind-set expands into collective mind-set (see Fig: 1).

---

[5] Ali A. Najam, *Listen:Brief Introduction to Rumi's Manavi Masnavi* (Islamabad: Agha Jee Printers, 2017)

Figure: 1Thoughtful Intelligence referred hierarchy of 'CHANGE'.

Thoughtful Change and the Individual
Thoughtful Change and the Community
Thoughtful Change and the Nation

Source: Self extract

Realization of gain and loss: The realization of gain and loss referred past sets the mind of thoughtful individual. The quality and quantity of realization depends on the feeling of gain & loss after the gain & loss of something of value[6].

II. Vision of thoughtfully intelligent individual

The vision should be clear and realistic regarding the physical and metaphysical part of the human life. The faculties are as follow:

Vision based on Knowledge of Oneness of the Creator: The thoughtful individual visualizes the fact of the oneness of Allah. "Prosperous are those who purify themselves, remember the name of their Lord, and pray[7]." The thoughtful individual visualizes the practice of 'Namaz'as the best prayer, the way to thank Allah. Medical Science Proved:

- Long prostration Sajda: Decreases heart problems. Increases eye sight, brain work and face beauty.
- Rukoo with straight legs: Reduces knees/joint problems.
- Straight standing after rukoo: Reduces Back bone problems.
- Muslim prayer improves digestive system, it is a full body tonic[8]

---

[6] One may say, "I feel a wonderful sense of gain" or "I feel a terrible sense of loss."

[7] Al-Quran, Al-Ala, Ayat:14-15

[8] **"Medical Benefits of Salat," accessed March 18, 2018,** http://www.islamicity.com

Iqbal says:

پھر دلوں کو یا د آ جائے گا پیغام سجود   پھر جبیں خاکِ حرم سے آشنا ہو جائے گی
The hearts will again recall the message of prostrations. The foreheads will become acquainted with the Harem's dust[9].

Vision based on Knowledge of Character of Prophet Muhammad (PBUH): The thoughtful individual visualizes Prophet Muhammad (PBUH) as the best personality model to follow. "The messenger of Allah is an excellent model for those of you who put your hope in Allah and the Last Day and remember him often[10]." Prophet Muhammad (PBUH) was the ever best leader. He is found on the *height of mercy*. He was lenient to *forgive* all misdeeds upon him for example the lady who threw daily garbage on him; when she got sick. The Prophet went to wish her health.

Iqbal says:

نگہ بلند سخن دل نواز جان پر سوز   یہی ہے رختِ سفر میر کارواں کے لیئے
High ambition, winsome speech, a passionate soul This is all the luggage for a leader of the Carvan[11].

Vision based on Knowledge of Righteousness: The thoughtful individual visualizes the knowledge of truthfulness, justice, and bravery.

Iqbal says:

سبق پھر پڑھ صداقت کا، عدالت کا م شجاعت کا   لیا جائے گا تجھ سے کام دنیا کی امامت کا
Read again the lesson of truth, of justice and valor! You will be asked to do the work of taking on responsibility for the world[12].

---

[9] Muhammad. Iqbal, **accessed March 18, 2018,** https://www.iap.gov.pk/
[10] Al-Quran Al-Ahzab, Ayat: 21
[11] Muhammad. Iqbal, **accessed March 18, 2018,** https://www.iap.gov.pk/
[12] Ibid

Vision based on Knowledge of Love: The thoughtful individual visualizes love among humanity, irrespective of cast and color. Being 'Loving' towards others simply makes you feel better. This is indeed the case, but there is another good reason all human beings have an inherent dignity, and your conscious choice to be a loving and kind person is a powerful way to honor that dignity. 'Ishq' is the term used for intense love, be it for humans or for the beauty of nature. Sometimes it can be related to abstract feelings like freedom, justice and so on. But the states and degrees of attachment, attractions or love are different. For example, a child's love for his mother is different in nature from a mother's love for her child. The love between husband and wife is yet different from those two. But all relationships between soul-entities have one common factor: they are two sided, mutual and interdependent. A two-sided relationship demands expression, manifestation and continued confirmation from both sides to keep alive and blossoming. One sided love would not yield union. The love between Allah and man is also two sided it cannot be that the Supreme Beloved would ever remain un-expressive and unresponsive to the supplication of worshipers[13].

Vision based on the Knowledge of Shaheen (Eagle) and Marde Momin (An ideal believer): The thoughtful individual visualizes the knowledge about Shaheen (Eagle) and Marde Momin (An ideal believer). Shaheen (Eagle) is a bird and used as a symbol (by Muhammad Iqbal in his poetry) of an ideal believer due to its certain traits: it has expansive vision, it has high flight, and it is self-reliant because it manages its own prey, contains self-respect, it does not confine to specific space and it is universal. It does not believe in specific abode as it likes highness and diversity.

Vision based on Knowledge of Nature: The thoughtful individual visualizes the knowledge of nature. "Ponder about nature: (Prophet), do you not see that Allah causes the night to merge into day and day to merge into night; that he has subjected to sun and the moon, each to run its course for a stated term, He (Allah) is aware of everything you (people) do[14]."

---

[13] Ali A. Najam, *Listen:Brief Introduction to Rumi's Manavi Masnvavi* (Islamabad: Agha Jee Printers, 2017), p. 193
[14] Al-Quran, Al-Luqman, Ayat: 29.

III. Self-assessment for thoughtful change

Self assessment is a process to realize and witness one's actions, attitudes, or performance. Each aspiring individual is obliged to go through a process of self-assessment.

"Truly man is a clear witness about himself.[15]." The self assessment must be designed to assess the intangible competencies; that can be loyalty, courage, humbleness, integrity, justice, identity, responsibility and self-governance. The loss of above qualities causes the downfall of the individual.

Iqbal says:

سبب کچھ اور ہے تو جس کو خو دیکھتا ہے   زوال بندہ مومن کا بے زری سے نہیں
With ease you can divine to something else is due: Penury can't cause decline of Muslims True[16].

Exercise
Track the vices inside you to establish your weaknesses
(see chapter 3). Track the virtues inside you to
establish your strengths (see chapter 3).

IV. Required individual competencies for a thoughtful change

The urge for change is the foremost requirement of change to approach thoughtful intelligence. The urge for change must be defined with righteousness and positive thinking. The Messenger of Allah (PBUH) said, "There is no *good* for me in a *day* that rises upon me and my knowledge does *not* increase that *day*[17]." Rasul Allah (PBUH) said: "He whose *two days* are equal, is a loser. He wants his inner self to be *better* today than it was yesterday and his tomorrow to be *better* than

---

[15] Al-Quran, Al-Qiama, Ayat: 14.

[16] Muhammad. Iqbal, accessed on 31 March 2018, https://www.iap.gov.pk/

[17] "Islamic center for research and academics," accessed March 5, 2018 http://icraa.org/hadith-whose-two-days-equal-loser.

today. Thus, a Momin's *two days* are *not* equal[18]. The following are linear changes to comprehend the thoughtful change.

1. No vagueness: Sensitivity to ambiguity and vagueness is essential to good thinking. There should be clarity in thought; e-g all the prophets argued that "Love for others" is one of the most important elements of humanity.
2. No pending - Do not say of anything, 'I will do that tomorrow[19].'
3. Commanding good & forbidding evil: Encourage positive actions and discourage the negative practices.
4. You can make the difference. A sparrow was asked, "How the drop in its beak can extinguish the fire meant for Abraham?" The sparrow replied that on the Day of Judgment my name would be in the list of fire fighters.
5. Commitment: "A fog can't be dispelled by a fan (fragile commitment)[20]." You have to work with commitment.
6. Self-Governance: To be self-controlled, avoiding extremes, and not to be excessively influenced or controlled by others[21].
7. Thoughtful word and action.

V. Required systematic competencies for thoughtful change

There are more chances of thoughtful change when it is appreciated by the immediate system (other individuals) around the individual. Two things are required; One is *father/mother's chastity* and the other is *father/mother's lawful earning.* Both of the things ensure righteous training of the children. As it is said, "People, eat what is good and lawful from the earth, and do not follow Satan's footsteps, for he is your sworn enemy"[22]. The system should have the following competencies.

---

[18] "Hadith explaination," accessed on March 5, 2018 http://dailyhadith.adaptivesolutionsinc.com/hadith/Are-Your-Two-Days-Equal.

[19] Al-Quran Al-Khaf, Ayat: 23.

[20] "30 awesome Japanese idioms we should start using in English," **accessed March 18, 2018,** https://matadornetwork.com/abroad/30-awesome-japanese-idioms-start-using-english.

[21] "Defining Civic Virtue: Launching Heroes & Villains with your Students," accessed Dec 16, 2016, http://billofrightsinstitute.org/wp-content/uploads/2014/10/What-is-Virtue-and-Franklin.

[22] Al-Quran, Al-Baqara, Ayat:168.

1. The system values social aspect of human personality.
2. The system competes for good actions.
3. The system appreciates good actions and condemns the bad actions.
4. The system urges to care the creatures.
5. The system mandates to generate profit for the community, nation and humanity.
6. The system extends Charity of thought & knowledge.
7. The system extends thoughtful word and action. The ultimate sense of giving is charity here I highlight free of money charity; it does not require money. Relish Table 2. 1.

VI. Automation of thoughtful change

With continuous practice you get automated. You need to deliberate RCC (Responsibility, Courage and Compassion) in all circumstances.

Responsibility: To strive to know and do what is best, not what is most popular. To be trustworthy for making decisions in the best long-term interests of the people and tasks of which they are in charge.

Courage: To stand firm in being a person of character and doing what is right, especially when it is unpopular or puts you at risk.

Compassion: To give and to forgive.

Moral: Change is the real deal!

Exercise

Think about how much cost free charity you are performing; start to perform all of them as per your status relevant to your family, community, and nation.

Table 2. 1 Free of Money Charity		
1.	Dua	Pray for people you care about and who asked you for prayer.
2.	Knowledge	Spread knowledge among those who cannot afford it.
3.	Advice	Give advice to your younger siblings or any who is younger than you.
4.	Smile	Meet people with a smiling face.
5.	Help	Help others to solve their problems.
6.	Time	Take time out for your parents and spouse.
7.	Nurturing	Nurture your children to be well mannered.
8.	Patience	Be always patient and rely on Allah.
9.	Remind	Remind your friends to stay on the righteous path.
10.	Forbid evil	Stop others from being harmful.
11.	Talk Softly	Do not be harsh and rude to your fellow humans.
12.	Forgive	Forgive the people who ask your forgiveness.
13.	Give respect	Give respect to elders as well as to youngsters.
14.	Be happy	Be happy and be happy for others and do not be jealous.
15.	Visiting the sick	Visit the sick; it is also the Sunnah of our beloved Prophet (PBUH).
16.	Clear the path	Remove harmful things such as a stone in the way.
17.	Feed your spouse	To put a piece of food into your wife's mouth[23].

Please rise to say:

**Allah increase me in righteous actions, Allah
grow me among righteous Caravans.**

---

[23] "17 Types Of Sadaqah That Don't Cost A Penny," accessed on March 10, 2018 http://www.muslimmastery.com.

CHAPTER 3

THOUGHTFUL INTELLIGENCE CLEANSES IN-SIDE OF THE INDIVIDUAL (TAZKIA-NAFS)

Thoughtful Intelligence initiates in-side cleansing: because the individual thrives from the in-side out. Chapter 3 hands on inner paradigm of the individual that establishes and defends moral values in the individual against internal and external threats. This defense includes detection, prevention and response to threats through the use of moral beliefs, values, rules and practices.

One of Khizra's junior got an opportunity to present her research paper in an International conference in Sri Lanka in 2001. Till that time no international conference had taken place in Khizra's academic life. She did not feel good to hear about her junior's conference participation. But she was able to detect the evil in her and wanted to prevent it. She struggled and tried to convince herself that she should not carry jealousy in her mind and art. Then she started to find out opportunities for her. She also started sharing the information with her colleagues. By following these two steps, she was able to earn two achievements. The first was the elimination of *jealousness* in her by knowing that she can have opportunity of participation in international conferences. The second was the elimination of *blame* that she put on her colleagues for not sharing the information of an international opportunity with her. Khizra's first exposure in international conference happened in 2003 in the Oxford University. Since then she presented her research papers in 40 well reputed international conferences. She also organized and headed the research panels in international conferences.

This day, Khizra counts the results of her *approach to thoughtful intelligence* for in-side cleansing regarding in-side evils of jealousness and blaming because her thinking capacity nurtured moral development in her and enhanced her connectivity in the system of humanity.

Khizra's mentor Qareeb advises, "If you feel the need of 'Greater Pilgrimage'; set out to travel infinite distances in-side you." I suggest inner journey to determine the in-side vices and virtues. This chapter describes the vices in-side the individual impeding the purity and highlights the virtues elating the purity.

    I. Edifice of purity
   II. In-side vices
   1. Arrogance
   2. Anger
   3. Vengefulness
   4. Lust

  III. In-side virtues
   1. Humbleness
   2. Love
   3. Kindness
   4. Modesty

  IV. Edify purity

I. Edifice of purity

The mind-set should be cleansed before serving the new style of thinking. The purity leads to thoughtful intelligence. Thoughtful intelligence has to do more with the inner understanding of outer practices that benchmarks and automates outer practices. To have and perform this strength the struggle is about in-side cleansing.

Prosperous are those who purify themselves[1].

Iqbal says:

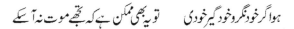

If the ego is self-preserving, self-creating and self-sustaining,
Then it is possible that even death may not make you die[2].

II. In-side vices

"Declare your jihad on twelve enemies you cannot see - Egoism, Arrogance, Conceit, Selfishness, Greed, Lust, Intolerance, Anger, Lying, Cheating, Gossiping and Slandering. If you can master and destroy them, then will be ready to fight the enemy you can see."[3] Here I focus four in-side evils; arrogance, anger, vengefulness and lust.

1. Arrogance

'Arrogance', is the mother of all evils which releases negative energy in-side and outside the human being. Arrogance means rejecting the truth and looking down on people. An arrogant person goes against the reality *of human dignity*.

Symptoms of arrogance: Proud and arrogant individual looks down upon others. He anticipates others to greet him and exhibit respect and deference towards him. A proud man will not tolerate any other to be on equal terms with him. In private and in public he expects that all should assume a respectful attitude towards him. They should acknowledge his superiority and treat him as a higher being. They should greet him first and make way for him wherever he walks. When he speaks everyone

---

[1] Al-Quran, Al-Ala, Ayat: 14

[2] Muhammad. Iqbal, accessed Sep 3, 2018, https://www.iap.gov.pk/

[3] Al-Ghazali, 'Quotes by Al Ghazali', accessed on 31 March 2018, https://www. goodreads.com

should listen to him and never try to oppose him. He thinks that he is a genius and people are like asses. They should be grateful to him, seeing that he is so lofty.

Arrogant thinking: Always nurturing aspects of his superiority and greatness within his mind and thinking that there is no need to change his arrogance.

Development of arrogance: Arrogance is one of the consequences of vanity and self-conceit. When an individual thinks too highly of himself, it is self-conceit; and when he tends, moreover, to consider others as inferior to him, that is arrogance. Arrogance is a mental state causing self-admiration and haughtiness against others in words or deeds. Arrogance is one of the most fatal of moral vices. This is so because arrogance is a thick veil which hides one's shortcomings from his own view and thus prevents him from removing them and attaining betterment.

Impact of arrogance: Pride and self-esteem lock him all. So long as man feels elated he will not like for others what he likes for himself. *His self-esteem will deprive him of humbleness, which is the essence of righteousness.* He will neither be able to discard enmity and envy, resentment and wrath, slander and scorn, nor will he be able to cultivate truth and sincerity, and attention to any advice. In short, there is no evil which a proud man will not inevitably do in order to preserve his elation and self-esteem.

Eradicating arrogance: The following way will help to eradicate arrogance. Holy Prophet Muhammad (SAW) says: "Even if you do not commit any sins, I fear that you may fall into something which is worse: pride! pride!" "Pride comes before the fall[4]." Imam Ali (AS) says: "I wonder at the arrogance of a haughty and vain person. Yesterday he was only a drop of semen and tomorrow he will turn into a corpse."

مت کرا تنافخر واپنے آپ پر انسان   نہ جانے خدانے کتنے تیرے جیسے بنا بنا کر مٹا دیئے

---

[4] "Proverbs 1 - New International Version (NIV) | Biblica" accessed July 10, 2018, https://www.biblestudytools.com/proverbs/

[5] Shayari, accessed on Sep 13, 2018 https://www.shayari123.com/hindi-shayari/mat-kar-itna-garoor-apne-aap-par-aye-insaan.html

> O man do't be proud;
> God erased many like you after creating[5]

What is envy? Not acceptance of good in others. If we accept that good it turns into inspiration.[6]

What is hatred? Not acceptance of person as he is---If we accept the person unconditionally----it becomes love.[7]

Exercise

Offer Namaz. Namaz is power that relieves a human from 'Arrogance.

2. Anger

Anger is an emotion characterized by antagonism towards someone or something you feel has deliberately done you wrong. Anger is an emotional response to a real or imagined threat or provocation. Anger can range in intensity from mild irritation to extreme rage. Anger is when one's blood boils confronted with a difficulty or with something unwanted. If one does not control himself in these situations he will seek revenge.

Significance of Anger: It is not necessarily a "bad" emotion. Anger makes people feel strong and powerful, which can motivate them to stand up for what they believe is *right*eous. Anger is both Merciful and Satanic. Anger can bring man to such a state that his angelic face will be turned into the face of a predatory animal. Anger must be used in the correct way. If a person uses anger in the animalistic way he will lose his angelic shape and turn into a predatory animal, but if he uses anger in the humane way he will become a perfect man, an example of good and full of blessings. Of course, man would not be able to live without anger. Considering all the obstacles in life, how would man be able to live without anger? But, if a man uses his anger in the animalistic way it will cause him to fall down from the state of humanity.

Anger management: Anger must be used in the correct way. Anger should occur when there is a barrier between him and improvement or perfection. One must become angry when another person wants to

---

[6] "Wisdom of Rumi", accessed December 2, 2017, https://steemit.comexposition
[7] Ibid

28

oppress him. What is meant by this is that he must not allow the other person to oppress him.

"Renunciation of the world is followed by peace; its desire brings sorrow. Retrain your desires, discipline yourself, and do not allow anyone to oppress your soul[8]."

Animalistic anger is the anger which is irrational. Whether it is anger or revenge, whenever it is against the intellect or against a religious law, it becomes animalistic. Suppose a person unintentionally hurt you, suppose he fell on you. If you get angry at him, curse him out and try to get revenge, you have used anger in the animalistic way. The person *unintentionally* hurt you he did not do it on purpose. An animal does not understand intentional and unintentional act so whenever something occurs that is against its will it gets angry. However a human being can understand if the other person hit him intentionally or unintentionally. The amount of anger that one has at oppression and sin, should be in relation to that form of oppression and sin. Some sins are bigger than others so the level of anger for those sins should be more as well. For example, these three sins are different, a woman having a little bit of her hair outside of her hijāb, a man drinking alcohol openly and a man killing an innocent person. The first sin is the smallest sin and the last one is the biggest. This holds true for seeking revenge as well. For example, you cannot do more than slap someone who slapped you or you cannot swear twice at someone who swore at you once. Of course, in any case it is better to forgive. There is a pleasure found in forgiving that is not found in revenge.

Moral: One must also be angry at those who create corruption, those who commit sins openly.

3. Vengefulness

Vengeance is a deep-seated dislike or ill will. Enmity suggests positive hatred which may be open or concealed. When a person is unforgiving, he is being vengeful. When you do not have faith in yourself

---

[8] "Rabi'a, 'Rabi's the Mystic," accessed July 2, 2014, http://www.beliefnet.com/inspiration

and trust in the creator, then you are being unforgiving and vengeful. When hatred shelters in hearts, kindness turns away.

Eradicating Vengefulness: The Quran mentions many times; that God is the most merciful and beneficent. In fact, all except one of the 114 chapters of the Quran begin, "With the name of God the Entirely Merciful and the Especially Merciful." These two descriptions of God are sometimes translated as 'the Compassionate the Merciful'. However in Arabic grammar, both names are an intensive form of the word 'merciful'.

Rehaman means merciful to all creation and justice is part of this mercy. Raheem means merciful especially to the believers and forgiveness is part of this mercy. A complementary and comprehensive meaning is intended by the use of both of them together. In addition Allah speaks of his forgiveness throughout the Quran. In fact, God's mercy and forgiveness have been mentioned together more than 70 times in the Quran.

4. Lust (temptation)

Lust is a strong emotion or feeling. The lust can take any form such as the lust for sex, lust for costly objects or the lust for power. It can take mundane forms such as the lust for food or it can become as distinct from the need of food.

Lust results in the continuation of human life. Lust and anger are two traits, two powers that Allah has put in-side the man. The continuation of mankind is dependent on these two traits. *Lust is used to attract benefits and anger is used to keep away the loss.* If one did not have any lust or desire he would not go after the things that his body needs. Man cannot live without anger or lust (*shahawat*). Man must have lust in him so that it will invoke in him the desire to go after food and marriage.[9] One would not eat if he did not have a desire for food, and when he does not eat he would die. So, it is a blessing that one has the desire for food that forces him to struggle to obtain something to eat. Sexual desires are also necessary for the prolongation of human life. Nobody would get married if sexual desires do not exist. Married life has its

---

[9] "Anger is both Merciful and Satanic," accessed on Oct 30, 2017, https://www.al-islam.org/islamic-ethics-ayatullah-dastaghaib-shirazi/lecture-7-anger-both-merciful-and-satanic.

difficulties and good & bad times. There must be a desire, a lust in man for him to marry and have children. Sexual desires are necessary for the continuation of human life. There should be rational realization of lust.

Determining the middle course is helped by the prevalent level of Thoughtful Intelligence in an individual. The middle course (*sirāt al-mustaqīm*) in religious matters means that a person should not be excessive, exceeding the limits set by Allah, the Almighty, the All-Powerful, nor be deficient, by not fulfilling what Allah, the Most Glorified, the Most High has ordained. An example of this is that a man says: I want to stand for the night prayer and I will not sleep any of the time, because prayer is one of the best forms of worship, so I love to spend all the night in prayer. This is excess in the religion of Allah, and it is not right, for something like this happened during the life of the Prophet Muhammad (PBUH). A number of people met and one of them said: I stand in prayer and I do not sleep, while another said: I fast and I do not break my fast, while a third said: I do not marry women. The Prophet Muhammad (PBUH) was informed of this and he Muhammad (PBUH) said: *"What is wrong with people who say such and such? I fast and I break my fast, I stand in prayer and I sleep and I marry women, so whoever dislikes my Sunnah is not from me*[10].*"*

---

[10] "TAWHEED FIRST," ACCESSED MARCH 18, 1018, https://tawheedfirst.wordpress.com/2009/06/21/the-middle-course

Table 3.1 Indicators of In-side Evils

1. *Jealousy: Jealousy* is an emotion. The term generally refers to the thoughts of insecurity, fear, concern, and envy over relative lack of possessions, status or something of great personal value, particularly in reference to a comparator. For example the jealous fellow_doesn't congratulate the other person's achievement.
2. *Cruelty: Cruelty* is pleasure acquired by inflicting suffering. Sadism can also be related to this form of action or concept. For example, *a sadist boss doesn't allow his subordinate to go on a leave* to have happy hours with his family and colleagues though the subordinate is entitled for holidays.
3. *Idleness:* Doing nothing for example *people sitting in apathetic tolerance of* corruption in the society and in highest levels of government.
4. *Aloofness:* Being disinterested for example the *educated citizenry in Pakistan do not cast vote* on the day of election and keep on sleeping.
5. *Inhospitality:* Unfriendly and unwelcoming towards people for example *people do not answer an invitation.*
6. *Self-centered:* Preoccupied with one's self and one's affairs for example, some people consider the opportunities only for themselves and *do not share.*
7. *Refusal:* A defense mechanism in which confrontation with a personal problem or with reality is avoided by *denying* the existence of the problem or reality. For example the individual refuses to acknowledge the *worth of a certain person in the system and ignores or rejects him.*

Source: Self extract

One's state in the hereafter depends on his state in this world. The person who falls off the middle course in this world will fall in the next world as well[11]. Albert Einstein wrote: "A calm and modest life brings more happiness than the pursuit of success combined with constant restlessness." The paper he wrote this quote on was sold for $1.3 million[12].

Moral: In-side evils impede contentment.

Exercise

Notice in yourself and others around you; that what is the level of in-side vices by using the liken indicators of in-side evils outside (See Table 3.1).

III. In-side virtues

Thoughtful intelligence can be struggled for and acquired. The growth of virtues has to face difficulty. In-side virtues are basic merits. Here I focus on humbleness, love, kindness, and modesty.

Iqbal says:

برا ہے سی نظر پیدا اکر مشکل سے ہوتی ہے
ہوس چھپ چھپ کے سینوں میں بنالیتی سے تصویریں

But it is difficult to create the insight of Abraham (A.S.);
Desire insidiously paints in our breasts[13].

1. Humbleness

In contrast to arrogance, when one thinks of himself as a small and insignificant being, that is called modesty; and when, in addition to this, he considers others as superior to himself, that is called humbleness. Humbleness is the quality of having a modest or low view of one's importance. The word 'humbleness' comes from the Latin root word

---

[11] Islamic Ethics,, accessed on Oct 31, 2017, https://www.al-islam.org/islamic-ethics-ayatullah-dastaghaib-shirazi/lecture-8-lust-results-continuation-human-life
[12] Albert Einstein's Quote about 'Living A Modest Life' sells for $1.3 Million, accessed on April 25, 2018, https://www.npr.org
[13] Muhammad. Iqbal, accessed on 31 March 2018, https://www.iap.gov.pk/

which means 'ground. Humbleness, or being humble, means that one is modest, submissive and respectful, not proud and arrogant.

Indicators of humbleness: The humble individual does not anticipate others to greet and respect him. A humble person thinks that others are equal to him. He never minds when he is not greeted by the others and only speaks when he is listened to. He lowers himself to the ground instead of elevating himself above others. While praying, Muslims prostrate themselves to the ground, acknowledging human beings' lowliness and humbleness before the Lord of the Worlds.

Humble thinking: Always nurturing aspects of his humbleness within his mind. Thinking that there is need to change is considered humbleness.

Impact of humbleness: Modesty and piety accelerate the idea to like the same for others as for one's self. A person's humbleness saves him from arrogance, which is hostile to righteousness. He will be able to disdain hostility, antagonism towards others.

Development of Humbleness: Humbleness is one of the consequences of selflessness and accepting the truth of timidity of man to the Lord of the worlds. When an individual thinks himself meek to the creator and aspires to connect with others to have his rights and to fulfill his duties, this entire act of his indicates humbleness. Humbleness is a mental state that compels a person to give to others through words and deeds. Humbleness is the apex virtue. Humbleness functions to highlight one's shortcomings and elates the capacity to move towards perfection.

Among the Jahliyya Arabs (before Islam), humbleness was unheard of. They preserved their personal honor above all else and would humble themselves to no one, neither a man nor a God. They were proud of their absolute independence and their human power. They had limitless self-confidence and refused to bow down to any authority. A man was lord of himself. Humbleness and submissiveness were considered weak traits - not a quality of a noble man. The Jahliyya Arabs had a fierce, passionate nature and would scorn anything which might make them humbled or humiliated in any way, or threatened their personal dignity and status.

Islam came and demanded of them, before anything else, to submit themselves wholly to the one and only Creator, and abandon all pride, arrogance, and feelings of self-sufficiency. Many among the pagan Arabs felt that this was an outrageous demand - to stand as equals with each other, in submission to Allah alone. For many, these feelings did not pass - indeed we still see them today in much of the world's people, and unfortunately, sometimes in ourselves. Human presumptuousness, insolence, arrogance, elevated self-worth, are around us everywhere. We have to fight it in our own hearts.

Bulleh Shah says:

چھلاں داتو عطر بنا   عطر اں دافر کڈ دریا

دریا وچ فررج کے نہا   مچھیاں وِنگوں تریاں لا

فیروی تیری بوُنہیں مکنی   پیلے اپنی میں نو مکا

Take out the essence of flowers and let it flow like a river.
Bath full well in the river of fragrance and swim like a fish.
But it won't remove your odor; till you kill the ego first[14].

Exercise

Ask other persons for help in decision making particularly you trust. Decentralize your powers while managing a task it could be a party at home or an official task. Asking others for help empowers you as others strength is connected to you. While thinking yourself not superior to others indicates your sense of connectivity to others particularly below to you; this sense of humbleness empowers you.

2. Love

Love is a feeling of fondness or tenderness for a person or thing based on attachment. Real love wheels on concepts, values and habits of cooperation and facilitation to create prosperity in the system of humanity. Love in Islam is an all-encompassing, comprehensive and sublime, rather than being restricted to one form only, which is the love between a man and a woman. There is love for Allah the Almighty, the Messenger of Allah (PBUH) the Companions of Allah's messenger (PBUH), may Allah be pleased with them, and the love of good and righteous people. There

---

[14] "Bulleh Shah Poetry," accessed on 31 July 2018, http://hamariweb.com/poetries/bulleh-shah_poetries

is love of the religion of Islam, upholding it and making it victorious and the love of martyrdom for the sake of Allah the Almighty as well as other forms of love. Consequently, it is wrong and dangerous to restrict the broad meaning of love to man and woman love only[15].

Indicators of love: Courage and commitment: "Courage is like muscle. We strengthen it with use[16]."

Appreciate Love thinking as in Table 3.2

Love thinking as in Table 3.2
1. Love yourself
2. Love your family
3. Love your institution
4. Love your community
5. Love your profession
6. Love your country
7. Love humanity

Impact of love: Love reduces stress, boosts immune health, relieves pain, and extends life.

Exercise

Meet yourself weekly by having food, dress and music of your choice. Meet yourself weekly by having food, dress and music of your family's choice.

3. Kindness

"A kind word is like spring day[17]." The more you are connected; the more you have sense of belonging that gives you the chance to get more love and give more love; the basic of kindness. Islam teaches Muslims to be kind to all of the God's creations, including their parents, relatives, neighbors, animals and the environment.

---

[15] "The concept of true love," accessed on Oct 31, 2017, https://www.islamweb.net/en/article/156581/the-concept-of-true-love-in-islam.

[16] Ruth Gordon, "Courage" accessed on 31 March 2018 https://www.goodreads.com

[17] Russian Proverb accessed on Oct 31, 2017, https://www.quotes.com

Parents: Kindness and respect towards parents is stressed throughout the Quran. The Quran says that you should honor your parents, speak with them respectfully and "lower to them the wing of humbleness, and say: 'My Lord! bestow on them thy Mercy even as they cherished me in childhood[18].'"

Children: Muslims strive to be like Prophet Muhammad (PBUH) and follow his examples. Many examples show the compassion Prophet Muhammad (PBUH) had for children, especially orphans.

Neighbors: In the Quran, Allah ordains for Muslims to do good to the "neighbors who are near" and the "neighbors who are strangers[19]." The Prophet said, "He is not a believer who eats his fill when his neighbor beside him is hungry" and "whose neighbors are not safe from his injurious conduct." He also said, "Whoever believes in Allah and the Day of Judgment should do good to his neighbor[20]."

Animals and the Environment: The Prophet said there is a reward for kindness to every living animal or human. He was tender and kind towards cats and often lowered his vessel to give cats a drink. In Islam, hunting birds and animals for pleasure or sport is not allowed. Hunting is only allowed as a means of sustenance. Similarly, Islam prohibits the cutting or destruction of trees and plants that yield fruit and, unless there is an absolute need for it.

Exercise

Make a weekly visit to the neighbors and *must* Eid visits to relations. Arrange water and meal for birds around your living place.

4. Modesty & Chastity

Lowering the gaze assures to manage the sexual lust. The sexual relationship must be declared and organized as per the morals of civilizations. The people known as unmarried couples; deviate dignity and responsibility called upon by human civilizations for male-female relationship. The attainment of young age by sons and daughters increases the responsibility of parents to arrange marriage for them. "When a man is blessed with a child, let him give his child a good

[18] Al Quran, Al-Isra, Ayat: 24
[19] "Top 11 Rights Neighbors Have On You", accessed October 31, 2017, https://www.zakat.org
[20] Ibid

name. He should bring him up on sound moral grounds and, when attains young age, the father must get him married. If the father fails to marry his son and he gets involved in any sin, the father will be held responsible for it[21]."

Exercise

Declare the relationship as life partners (wife and husband) against the concept of boy friend and girl friend.

Table 3. 3 Indicators of In-side Virtues

1. *Content:* State of satisfaction but trying to change the things around you; which may impact the level of existing satisfaction. The face of an individual with contentment shows the rest in-side and he *realizes the hardships of others.*

2. *Generosity:* Open handedness to spread bounty. The *knowledgeable spreads* his knowledge without discriminating the persons.

3. *Forgiving: Forgiveness* is the act of pardoning an offender. *You forgive* the person who hurts you.

4. *Patience:* Patience is the quality of being patient, as the bearing of provocation, annoyance, misfortune, or pain, without complaint, loss of temper, irritation, or the like. For example, the *widow rears and cares wholeheartedly* for her children without complaining the loss of her husband.

5. *Adaptability: Adaptability* shows the ability to learn from experience. For example, the *daughter/son in law adapts* his/her in-laws style of life.

6. *Hospitality:* Friendly treatment of visitors and guests for example, you *answer the invitation.*

7. *Confession:* Admitting that one is guilty of an offense for example, you say sorry and admit your mistake.

Moral: In-side virtues enhance contentment.

Exercise

Notice in yourself and the others around you; that what is the level of in-side virtues by using the liken indicators of in-side virtues outside (See Table 3.3).

Scaling Purity: Now you can think to scale the growth pattern of impurity and purity in you to eliminate impurity in you (see Figure 1).

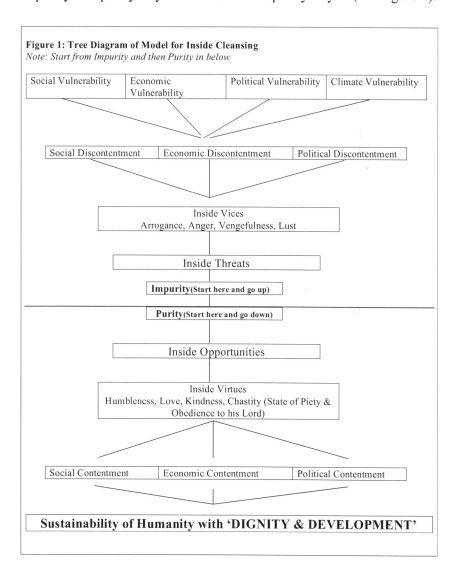

Figure 1: Tree Diagram of Model for Inside Cleansing
Note: Start from Impurity and then Purity in below

| Social Vulnerability | Economic Vulnerability | | Political Vulnerability | Climate Vulnerability |

| Social Discontentment | Economic Discontentment | Political Discontentment |

Inside Vices
Arrogance, Anger, Vengefulness, Lust

Inside Threats

Impurity(Start here and go up)

Purity(Start here and go down)

Inside Opportunities

Inside Virtues
Humbleness, Love, Kindness, Chastity (State of Piety & Obedience to his Lord)

| Social Contentment | Economic Contentment | Political Contentment |

Sustainability of Humanity with 'DIGNITY & DEVELOPMENT'

It is your decision—that you choose vices or virtues
to program your mind-set. Iqbal says:

> پرواز ہے دونوں کی اسی ایک ہی فضا میں
>
> کرکس کا جہاں اور ہے شاہیں کا جہاں اور

The vulture and the eagle soar
In the same air, but in worlds apart[22].

IV. Edify purity

"Others read your face, God reads your heart[23]." The book offers
you the way to edify purity. When we start with Bismila we start to
locate our relationship towards Rehman-o-Rahim that what we can
have? What we can do? If we commit certain mistakes we would be
forgiven. Get out of your way, be not the hurdle so as to be closer to the
ever merciful.

Hazrat Ali (A.S) says:

> اپنی سوچوں کو پانی کے قطروں سے بھی زیادہ شفاف رکھو کیونکہ جس طرح پانی
>
> کے قطروں سے دریا بنتا ہے اس طرح سوچوں سے ایمان بنتا ہے (حضرت علی)

Keep your thoughts transparent like water drops because the
drops compose river; likewise thoughts compose belief[24].

How to establish and enhance Purity? "Truly it is in the remembrance
of God where hearts find peace[25]."

- Remembrance of God in thoughts
- Remembrance of God in words
- Remembrance of God in actions

---

[22] Muhammad. Iqbal, accessed July 6, 2018,, https://www.iap.gov.pk/

[23] "Slovakian Proverb," accessed on Oct 31, 2017, https://www.quotes.com

[24] "Hazrat Ali Quotes," accessed on May 13, 2018, https://www.google.com.pk/hazrat+ali+quotes

[25] Al-Quran, Al-Raad, Ayat: 28

When each thought and action is as per style appreciated by Allah and the Prophet Muhammad (PBUH) than each thought and action leads to contentment. "They will enter perpetual Gardens graced with flowing streams. There they will have everything they wish. This is the way God rewards the RIGHTEOUS[26]." To offer Namaz is a noble deed; now if it is value added as follows, you will advance in purity:

- Ablution as practiced by Prophet Muhammad (PBUH)
- Clean place
- Wearing clothes earned through legitimate sources
- Love of Allah almighty
- Love of Prophet Muhammad (PBUH)

Exercise

Count on that how many thoughts compose your intention while planning some action? The purity is classified with the Taqwa. Explain and instill Taqwa in you and in your companions as follows:

"What is Taqwa?

Taqwa is not about looking Islamic.

Taqwa is not about sporting a beard or wearing a Hijab.

Taqwa is not about appearance.

BUT

Taqwa is when you miss a prayer, you feel uneasy the whole day.

Taqwa is when you speak a lie, you feel bad.

Taqwa is the guilt that follows when you hurt someone knowingly or unknowingly.

Taqwa is the shame and regret that follows a sin you committed knowing full well how it stands in the sight of Allah.

Taqwa is when you cannot sleep after disobeying or disrespecting your parents.

Taqwa is to cry in the depths of night fearing none but the one above the Arsh.

Taqwa is the fear that constrains you from sinning when nobody familiar is around.

---

[26] Al-Quran, Al-Nahal, Ayat: 31

Taqwa is the guts and the will to please Allah, even when the whole world is hell bent on displeasing Him.

Taqwa is to wear that beard and Hijab for the sole reason of pleasing our Creator and to keep it on as per Sunnah..

Taqwa is to stay happy and smiling, knowing that this world is a prison for believers.

Taqwa is the good manners and character we practice for the sake of Allah.

Taqwa is the struggle to better ourselves according to Islam, with each passing day."[27]

Here I suggest you to stick onto Thoughtful intelligence that is the higher order of thinking to train the mind-set to produce intentions and actions. Thoughtful intelligence can be struggled for and acquired. It is comprised of capacity to understand and realize the impact of one's thoughts, words and actions on others' (individuals', groups', and nations') survival, dignity[28] and development in time (days, weeks, months or years) and space (geographical land with or without human beings). It establishes thoughtful thoughts. Per the inner paradigm[29]: Thoughtful intelligence establishes and defends moral values in the individual against internal and external threats. This defense includes detection, prevention and response to threats through the use of moral beliefs, values, rules and practices. Thoughtful intelligence visions the eyes to observe and gives the courage[30] to understand befittingly suited to difficult times; and reveals compassion[31] for moral development.

Please rise to say:

May we are able to have in-side purity based on compassion and mercy leading to contentment that is ultimate goal of humanity.

---

[27] "Taqwa" accessed Sep 19, 2018, https://www.instagram.com/taqwa
[28] Al-Quran, Bani Israel, Ayat :70 'And We have certainly honored the children of Adam'
[29] The inner paradigm is a framework containing all the accepted views of an individual about human life (past, present, and future); inclusive social, economic, political, and security dimensions.
[30] Courage is the ability to do something that frightens one: bravery.
[31] Compassion is the ability to give and to forgive.

CHAPTER 4

THOUGHTFUL INTELLIGENCE PARKS THOUGHTFUL THOUGHTS

Thought is an idea or opinion produced by thinking. It is the action or process of thinking. Once Khizra was discussing the concept of 'Sustainable decision making' with her Executive Director. Khizra argued that decisions should be benchmarked with thoughtfulness. She encountered the argument that every decision has a thought but she continued her case that each decision can have a thought but not a *thoughtful thought.*

Thoughtful intelligence is the higher order of thinking to train the mind-set to produce intentions and actions. Thoughtful intelligence can be struggled for and acquired. It is comprised of capacity to understand and realize the impact of one's thoughts, words and actions on others' (individuals', groups', and nations') survival, dignity[1] and development in time (days, weeks, months or years) and space (geographical land with or without human beings). It establishes thoughtful thoughts. Per the inner paradigm[2]: Thoughtful intelligence establishes and defends moral values in the individual against internal and external threats.

---

[1] Al-Quran, Bani Israel, Ayat: 70 'And We have certainly honored the children of Adam'
[2] The inner paradigm is a framework containing all the accepted views of an individual about human life (past, present, and future); inclusive social, economic, political, and security dimensions.

<u>This defense includes detection, prevention and response to threats</u> <u>through the use of moral beliefs, values, rules and practices. Thoughtful</u> <u>intelligence visions the eyes to observe and gives the courage[3] to</u> <u>understand befittingly suited to difficult times; and reveals compassion[4]</u> <u>for moral development.</u>

Khizra's mentor Qareeb shows his concern about the moral development in the premises of globalization[5] through high-tech media[6]. The kind and quality of thoughts being boosted over the young mind-sets lead to unlimited mental and material pursuits.

The scenario challenges the capacity of the youth to process the information available to respond because they are connected with the two societies; a society where they exist actually and the other where they are connected virtually. A *thoughtful individual knows the diverse modes of discourse* in the sciences, social sciences and humanities. He knows the indifferent discourses the people define.... debate and solve the problems. Thoughts structure the vision; where there are no thoughts people perish. Furthermore the mode and style of thought matters.

---

[3] Courage is the ability to do something that frightens one: bravery.
[4] Compassion is the ability to give and to forgive.
[5] Globalization processed by fast communication has signed thoughtless language, and thoughtless relations, through social media among the peoples. It has infected distortions in the family institution, and mental garbage across the societies.
[6] "When asked what one did over the weekend, we often hear the boast, 'Oh, I binge-watched Game of Thrones' or one of the other numerous series of cluttering the airwaves. Coupled with other online distractions like play stations and social media, the opportunity for healthy mental pursuits is almost non-existent. Since we do not study history and literature or study science and technology, our mental faculties are not being developed to their potential. As a result, we can't debate with any sense of authority, nor can we see beyond the surface of an issue. Our reactions are usually knee-jerk as we lack any background knowledge of national or world affairs. Make sure you are staying away from 'junk food for the mind' and are following a healthy reading 'exercise' plan with lots of mind games thrown in. Junk food leads to diabetes and obesity, junk food for the mindset can be worse." Daily DAWN, accessed Sep 2018, https://epaper.dawn.com

Iqbal says:

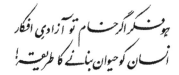

Free thinking can bring about the ruin of those
whose thoughts are low and mean:
They don't possess the mode and style of
thought that may be chaste and clean.

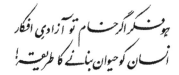

If thoughts are raw and immature no good accrues to man in least:
The utmost that such thoughts can do is
change of man to state of beast[7].

Here I present the thoughtful thoughts in seven perspectives.

    I. Sustainability thought
   II. Nature's thought
  III. Social thought
  IV. Economic thought
   V. Political thought
  VI. Justice thought
 VII. Global thought

So far over three chapters you have enhanced your ability to cleanse inside. This chapter is *intersection* between the earlier three chapters and later three chapters. To struggle thoughtful intelligence thoughtful thoughts should park in the mind. Now from inner travel I interlock you to outer travel through the thoughts which you may bereft with the external travel to connect to ultimate being of the unlimited universe composed of past-present and future. Iqbal's following couplet gives us strength to concrete thoughtful thoughts in this chapter.

---

[7] Muhammad. Iqbal, accessed Sep 2, 2017, https://www.iap.gov.pk/

Iqbal says:

جُرأت ہے تو افکار کی دنیا سے گزر جا

میں بحر خودی میں ابھی پوشیدہ جزیرے

Transcend the intellect if you have courage to do so: There
are islands hidden in the ocean of the self as yet.

کُھلتے نہیں اس قلزم خاموش کے اسرا

جب تک تو اسے ضرب کلیمی سے نہ چیرے

The secrets of this silent sea, however, do not yield
until you cut with blow of the Moses' rod[8].

I. Sustainability thought

How can/should we ensure our sustainability?

A person exists to the extent of his deeds. Each individual believes
that a day of expiry will come. The real belongings are the deeds. The
deeds survive as per quantity of practices by the heirs[9]. Thoughtful
intelligence enhances the capacity to understand and realize the impact
of one's thoughts, words and actions on others' (individuals', groups',
and nations') survival, dignity[10] and development in time (days, weeks,
months or years) and space (geographical land with or without human
beings). Deeds make the man immortal.

Iqbal says:

ہوا گر خود نگر و خود گیر خودی   تو یہ بھی ممکن ہے کہ تجھے موت نہ آ سکے

If the ego is self-preserving, self-creating and self-sustaining,
Then it is possible that even death may not make you die[11].

---

[8] Muhammad. Iqbal, accessed Sep 2, 2017, https://www.iap.gov.pk/
[9] The heirs are not the legal ones; but everybody doing the same practices as of the expired.
[10] Al-Quran, Bani Israel, Ayat:70 'And We have certainly honored the children of Adam'
[11] Muhammad. Iqbal, accessed Sep 2, 2017, https://www.iap.gov.pk/

Sustainability thought depends on: Faith in the unseen, Faith in the finality of Prophet-hood, and Faith in the hereafter.

Faith[12] in the unseen and the life hereafter: "This is the scripture in which there is no doubt, containing guidance for those who are mindful of God, who believe in the unseen, keep up the prayers and give what we have provided for them; those who believe in the revelation sent down to you (Muhammad) and what was sent before you, those who have firm faith in the hereafter. Such people are following their Lord's guidance and it is they who will prosper[13]."

Iqbal says:

> خودی کا سر نہاں لا الٰہ الا اللہ
>
> خودی ہے تیغ فساں لا الٰہ الا اللہ
>
> The secret of the Self is hid, In words "No God but Allah alone".
> The Self is just a dull-edged sword, "No
> God but He", the grinding stone[14].

The Hereafter is for one who does not seek superiority: It is self-evident that an ignorant person will not benefit from the next world's positions because: ***"Are those who know equal to those who do not know[15]?"*** The scholars are the ones who always remember Allah. This world will remain more important than the hereafter to an ignorant person.

Iqbal says:

> یقین پیدا کر اے نادان یقین سے ہاتھ آتی ہے   وہ درویشی کہ جس کے سامنے جھکتی ہے فغفوری
>
> O fellow stupid, get firm belief, For faith upon you can bestow
> Dervishhood of such lofty brand, For which
> the mighty monarchs bow[16].

---

[12] Faith means trust, confidence, assurance and belief.

[13] Al-Quran Al-Baqra, Ayat: 2-5

[14] Muhammad. Iqbal, accessed Sep 2, 2017, https://www.iap.gov.pk/

[15] Al-Quran Al-Zumar, Ayat: 9

[16] Muhammad. Iqbal, accessed Sep 2, 2017, https://www.iap.gov.pk/

Moral: Good deeds ensure the sustainability of each individual.

Exercise

Always keep on observing that what impact your each thought, word and action will create in your life and after your death.

II. Nature's thought

How can/should we connect to nature/natural resources?

Nature impacts the human thoughts. Nature is the most beautiful and precise. The sunrise constantly reminds us of our pact with the nature. In the morning the individual should glow and be generous like the sun. In the evening the individual should moderate and be kind like the moon.

Plato's theory of knowledge – his epistemology – can best be understood through thinking about beauty[17]. We are born with all knowledge, he says, but when our soul became trapped in our body at birth, we forgot this knowledge. Learning, then, is similar to remembering. And here on earth, beauty is the easiest way for us to first do that. We can all recognize individual beautiful things... flowers, sunsets, music, people. Recognizing these things is the first rung on the ladder to the *knowledge of Beauty*, which for Plato is the Ideal form of Beauty. Recognizing these individual beautiful things is the world we all live in most of the time.

The question then is; whether there is something in common that makes all of these things beautiful? The next step is recognizing what all beautiful things share in common. What they have in common is the 'Ideal Form of Beauty'. The top rung of the ladder, 'true wisdom' is to know Beauty.

Buckle had tried to write the history of human civilization in the light of scientific knowledge to fashion a few 'laws' based on inclusive reasoning, for example the law of seasons that showed that the physical environment greatly affected human culture[18]. The earliest recording

---

[17]

[18] Henry. Thomas Buckle, *History of Civilization in England* (Cambridge: Cambridge University Press, 2012.

of the 7th Generation[19] principle dates back to the 'Great Law of Peace of the Iroquois Confederacy' created in the 12th Century. When US Founding Fathers looked for the examples of effective government and human liberty upon which to model a Constitution to unite the thirteen colonies, they found it in the government of the Iroquois Nation, which stood for hundreds of years. The "7th generation[20]" principle taught by Native Americans says, "Every decision, be it personal, governmental or corporate, we must consider how it will affect our descendents seven generations into the future. So that the pristine sky, field and mountains in the photo still be there for them to enjoy". Long before environmentalists got thinking about "carbon footprints" and "sustainability," indigenous peoples lived in balance with the world around them. Ironically, in drafting US constitution, the founders left out one of the essential principles of the Great Law of Peace: the 7th Generation principle.

Prophet Muhammad (PBUH) says:

> "إِنَّ اللهَ جَمِيلٌ يُحِبُّ الْجَمَالَ"

Allah is beautiful He loves beauty.

---

[19] The Seventh Generation Principle, https://www.mollylarkin.com/what-is-the-7th-generation-principle-and-why-do-you-need-to-know-about-it-3/

[20] Western society generally considers a generation to be 25 years; the Lakota Nation considers one generation to be 100 years

Quran says:

وَسَخَّرَ لَكُم مَّا فِي السَّمَاوَاتِ وَمَا فِي الْأَرْضِ جَمِيعًا مِّنْهُ إِنَّ فِي ذَلِكَ لَآيَاتٍ لِّقَوْمٍ يَتَفَكَّرُونَ
"And He has subjected to you, as from Him, all that is in the heavens and on earth: Behold, in that are Signs indeed for those who reflect[21]."

May you have always have walls for the wind, a roof for the rain, tea beside the fire, laughter to cheer you. Those you love near you, and for every storm, fascinating heavenly rainbow[22].

Moral: Nature/Beauty is the easiest place to start the road towards 'Knowledge' of thoughtful intelligence.

Exercise

What is the most beautiful thing you've ever seen? Share a picture along with your explanation in the comments with your friends and family. Get inspiration from nature: Nothing in nature lives for itself. Rivers don't drink their water. Trees don't eat their own fruit. The sun doesn't shine for itself. A flower's fragrance is not for itself. Living for each other is the rule of nature. Watch scenic beauty before going to bed; you would have beautiful dreams.

III. Social thought

How can/should we relate to human resources?

Social relationships refer to the connections that exist between people who have recurring interactions that are perceived by the participants to have personal meaning. This includes relationships between family members, friends, neighbors, co-workers, and other associates. A person is known to the extent of his style of behavior with parents, sisters/brothers, neighbors, and opposite sex in paradigms of appreciation and condemnation leading to purity.

Basic questions to construct relational senses

---

[21] Al-Quran, Al-Jathiyah, Ayat:13
[22] "Irish blessing" accessed Sep 13, 2018 https://www.pinterest.com

- What task do you give to your eyes to see?
- What task do you give to your ears to listen?
- What task do you give to your hands to do?

Quran says, "How prosperous are the believers. Those who pray humbly, who shun idle talk, who pay the prescribed alms, who guard their chastity except with their spouses. Who are faithful to their trusts and pledges and who keep up their prayers will rightly be given paradise as their own. There to remain[23]."

The Prophet (PBUH) says:

> بَابُ الْمُسْلِمِ مَنْ سَلِمَ الْمُسْلِمُونَ مِنْ لِسَانِهِ وَيَدِه
>
> "A Muslim is the one who avoids harming Muslims with his tongue and hands[24]."

Exercise

Refrain idle talk. Guard chastity. Refrain from back biting. Refrain spying: Quran says, Believers avoid too many assumptions –some assumptions are sinful and do not spy on one another or speak ill of people behind their backs.

Family: The first ever relationship was of wife and husband. The desire to touch the opposite sex is human. One should not refrain from marriage because this has been ordered against. The Prophet of Islam says, "Marriage is a good custom (*sunnah*) and something that I have done. One who does not act according to my customs is not from me[25]." Refraining from marriage all together is a form of negligence. It is necessary for one's soul to make a family. One finds perfection after dealing with the difficulties of marriage and childbearing. Religious decrees are related to man's nature and instincts. One who acts in excess or refrains from satisfying his desires is not only acting against the divine orders but he also suffers from spiritual and physical diseases.

---

[23] Al Quran, Sura Al Mminune, Ayat :1-11
[24] "Religion and Spirituality", accessed June 3, 2018, https://www.sunnah.com
[25] Ibid

He loses the blessings of having a household which provides him with a satisfaction not only on physical level but also on the spiritual level.

Unmarried couples: The people known as unmarried couples deviate from dignity and responsibility called upon by the human civilizations for male female relationship. They enjoy the relationship without responsibility and get frustrations for rest of the life.

Romantic and Real Love: Commenting on this phenomenon, Professor Saul Gordon, said, "When you are in love; to you the whole world revolves around this person whom you love. Marriage then comes to prove the opposite and destroy all your perceptions. This is because you discover that there are other worlds that you have to be aware of. It is the world of humans, *the world of concepts, values and habits to which you have paid no attention before.*" "Romantic love is very strong and emotional, but does not last, while real love[26] is linked to real life and can withstand trials." Real love means sharing the concerns of daily life and cooperation for it to continue. Within the framework of this cooperation, one can achieve his human need. "Real love" has been expressed in the Quran as affection. Allah the Exalted says, *"And of His Signs is that He created for you from yourselves mates that you may find tranquility in them; and He placed between you affection and mercy[27]."* The relationship between spouses is based on affection and mercy, not on ardent love, desire and passion. It is a relationship which is based on quiet love (affection) and mutual mercy, not illusions of love which fail to withstand reality or romantic fantasies which fail to create a successful marriage. The Messenger of Allah, (PBUH), gave us the best example of loving his wives. It was narrated in the pure *Sunnah* (tradition) that the Prophet, (PBUH), was careful to put his mouth on the same place of the bowl from which his wife 'Aa'ishah, may Allah be pleased with her, drank. During his final illness, he used her *Siwaak* (tooth stick) and died while he was reclined against her chest, between her neck and bosom. What kind of love is nobler and more sublime than this[28]."

---

[26] The concept of true love in Islam, accessed on Dec 18, 2017, https://www.islamweb.net
[27] Al-Quran, Al-Rum, Ayat: 30-21
[28] "The concept of true love," accessed on Oct 31, 2017, https://www.islamweb.net/en/article/156581/the-concept-of-true-love-in-islam.

Friendship: The thought and art can't survive if it is not appreciated by the on hand system. For Aristotle, friendship is one of the most important virtues in achieving the goal of eudaimonia (happiness). ... Aristotle calls it a "... complete sort of friendship between people who are good and alike in virtue[29]" Quran says, "Content yourself with those who pray to their Lord in morning and evening, seeking his approval, and do not let your eyes turn away from them out of desire for the attractions of this worldly life[30]."

Societal Dignity: Indicators of soocietaldignity can be noticed when: People like to sit with you. People like to consult you. People share with you.

Tools to acquire societal dignity: I present the following tools to acquire social dignity that is 'The Wealth of Humanity'.

a) Dignifying others	b) Appreciation	c) Confession

Dignifying others: All human beings have an inherent dignity. Your conscious choice to be a loving and kind person is powerful way to honor that dignity. Being loving is an ideal to which we should aspire.

Iqbal says:

آدمیت احترام آدمی   با خبر شو از مقام آدمی
Humanity means respect of the mankind- learn to appreciate the true worth of man.

"Look at the world through other person's eye. In the 1989 film 'Dead Poet Society' the new teacher Jhon Keeting (played by Robin William's) asked each student stand up on his desk and look at the world from a new perspective.

Ask for help. During my workshops, I ask for volunteers to present ethical problems they are facing, because the collective wisdom in the room can provide solutions they wouldn't have thought of on their own.

---

[29] "Friendship For Aristotle Friendship Is..." accessed October 31, 2017, https://www.coursehero.com.

[30] Al-Quran, Al-Kahf, Ayat:28

It also helps when someone says, "this happened to me, and here it is how I handled it." It is good to know you are not alone.

Being kinder to your-self makes it easier to be kinder to others. The converse is also true, as Mark Twain noted: "the best way to cheer yourself up is to try to cheer somebody else up.

You are better off not making enemies and wasting your energy. I have found that having hateful feelings toward people who have wronged me does nothing to them but a lot of damage to me. Better to set those feelings aside and focus on better, more important things[31]"

Appreciation: Recognition and enjoyment of the good qualities of someone or something (see Table 4. 1 Ideas to Establish Appreciation).

Table 4.1 Ideas to Establish Appreciation
1. Thanks that you exist in a social system where good deeds are encouraged.
2. Thanks the blessings you have when you find the others deprived.
3. Take into account the number of blessings that other people around you have. How can you contribute into that?
4. Take into account that how much the misery the others have around you. How can you eradicate them?
5. To love something and then to live up with the loss of the same thing is also a kind of appreciation.
6. Praise the other person in front of others and condemn/suggest in lone.
7. When the other sneezes you say Alhamdullilah, that means you are giving thanks to Allah.
Source: Self extract

---

[31] Wienstein, Bruce. *Ethical Intelligence: Five Principles for Untangling Your Toughest Problems at Work and Beyond.* (California: New World Library, 2013).

Exercise

Appreciate God for everything you have. Write down 10 things you have in your life that give you happiness. Focus on the good/positive things!

Confession: Confession is a statement claiming that one is guilty of wrong doing. Quran says, "God loves those who repent and turn to Him[32]." You are right the moment you feel you were wrong (see Table 4. 2 *Ideas to Establish Confession*).

Table 4. 2 Ideas to Establish Confession

1. Feel sorry if somebody is hurt by your thought.
2. Feel sorry if somebody is hurt by your words.
3. Feel sorry if somebody's belonging is hurt by you.
4. Feel sorry for the bad deeds around you.
5. Feel sorry for others deprivation. How can you eradicate that?
6. Feel sorry that the prayer you have offered is not at par and keep on trying to improve.
7. Lest somebody falls try to support the fallen person.

Source: Self extract

Moral: Dignify humanity.

Exercise

Repent everything you have done wrong to yourself, and to your relations in family, friends, neighbors or coworkers and in the bad interest of humanity; knowingly or unknowingly. Think to refer your personal and collective goals to the system of humanity. Think to be in the well wishes of others; as the well wishes excel you.

---

[32] Al-Quran, Al-Baqara, Ayat: 222

IV. Economic thought

How can/should we participate in the economic activity?

Economics is about managing unlimited desires and limited means. Khizra's mentor *Qareeb is* concerned that how the homes are turning into houses and houses into warehouses. That indicates the moral bankruptcy of the nations and humanity. A person is also known to the extent of his style of economic behavior in spending on humanity and utilizing private ownership for public good?

Quran says, "This is a scripture in which there is no doubt, containing guidance for those who are mindful of God, who believe in the unseen, keep to the prayer, and give out of what we have provided for them those who believe in the revelation sent down to you (Muhammad), and in what was sent before you, those who have firm faith in the hereafter. Such people are following their Lord's guidance and it is they who will prosper[33]," "People, eat what is good and lawful from the earth, and do not follow Satan's footsteps, for he is your sworn enemy[34]."

Guidelines for economic thought and practice

- Quran says, "In consumption, there is a responsibility principle that everything consumed will impact human physique and behavior[35]."
- Conduct permissible enterprise (permissible conduct) afar from riba/usury[36].
- The implementation of zakat that is compulsory and sadaqah, wakaf, hadiah/gift donated voluntarily have an effect towards the behavior of Muslim consumer.
- Abstain from wasteful and luxurious living; that the economic activity should be to fulfilling the needs and not satisfying the greed.

Thoughtful consumption is about planning to consume the least to fulfill the material needs of life dependent on natural resources.

---

[33] Al-Quran, Al-Baqara, Ayat: 1-5
[34] Al-Quran, Al-Baqara, Ayat:168
[35] Al-Quran, Al-Mulk, Ayat: 15)
[36] "INTERPRETATION OF VERSES ON CONSUMPTION," accessed on Dec 18, 2017, http://journal.uii.ac.id/index.php/Millah/article/viewFile/430/344

Informal tools of thoughtful consumption
- *Generosity:* "To limit the needs is wealth." Imam Zain ul Abideen
- *Patience* leads to demand management: Restraining water usage is application of patience.

Formal tools of thoughtful consumption
Zakat is payment made annually under Islamic law on certain kinds of property and used for charitable and religious purposes, one of the Five Pillars of Islam.

Moral: Minimize the needs to use of resources/natural resources.

Exercise

- *Spend your money on experiences.* A study found that 75% of people felt happier when they invested their money in travel, learning courses and classes; only 25% said they felt happier while buying things.
- *Conserve energy and water.* Scaling the energy conservation literacy ask the following qualitative questions to yourself and others:

Would you like to reduce energy consumption for *helping the society* as the energy you save can be used by others?
Would you like to reduce energy consumption for *helping the future generations* as the energy you conserve can be used by next generations?
How would you like to *respond to energy crises of Pakistan* in your personal capacity?

V. Political thought

How can/should we participate in the political activity?
Political thought is about cause and effect of *decisions made by the politicians.* The individual is accountable as voter while polling to elect political representatives. The political representatives decide the allocation of natural and human resources while implying the survival and the dignity of the individual and the nation. A person is also known

to the extent of his style of political behavior based on the prevalent political system to appreciate the good governance and condemn the bad governance and corruption.

Distortions in the political system generate corruption that is the high factor in de-characterizing a nation. The annual Corruption Perceptions Index, released by Transparency *International* (TI), has *ranked Pakistan* number 116 of 176 countries that were included in the index for the year 2016[37]. "When exposing a crime is treated as committing a crime, you are ruled by criminals[38]."

Chinese Wisdom; Back in the third century A. D the Chinese king sent his son Prince Tai to a temple to get education from the great master Pan Ku. Prince Tai was to succeed his father as king. Pan Ku was to teach the boy the basics of being a good ruler. When the prince arrived at the temple, the master sent him alone to the Ming Li Forest with the advice to meditate and discover the various sounds in the forest. After a year, the prince was to return to the temple to submit his findings of the sounds before the great master.

When prince Tai returned, Pan Ku the great master at the temple asked the boy to describe all that he had seen and heard during stay in the forest.

Respected master, "said the prince, "I could hear the cuckoos sing, the leaves rustle, the humming birds hum that crickets chirp, the grass blow, the bees buzz, and the winds whisper." When the prince had narrated all that he had experienced, the master ordered him to go back to the forest again. He told him to stay there for another year to listen to what more he could hear. The prince was puzzled by the master's new order". Had he not already discerned every sound and explained everything to the master." thought the prince.

He went back to the forest again for one year more with the advice to meditate and discern various sounds in the forest.

For many days and nights, the young prince sat alone in the forest listening to the sounds more attentively. But he heard no sounds other

[37] DAWN, "Little Change in Pakistan's Ranking in Corruption Index" accessed February 23, 2018, https://www.dawn.com/news/1391129
[38] Gillespie, Nick. "When Exposing a Crime is Treated as Committing a Crime, You Are Ruled By Criminals.", accessed on 31 March 2018, http://www.reason.com

than the ones he had already heard. Then, one morning, as the prince sat silently beneath the trees, he started to discern faint sounds unlike those he had ever heard before. The more closely he listened, the more audible and clearer the sounds became. The feeling of enlightenment enveloped the boy.

"These must be the sounds the master wished me to discern."

He reflected. When Prince Tai returned to the temple, the master asked him what more he heard. "Respected master," responded the prince reverently, "when I listened most closely, I could hear the unheard sound of flowers' opening, the sound of the sun's warming the earth and the sound of the grass with the morning dew."

The master nodded approvingly:

"To hear the unheard, "remarked Pan Ku, "is a necessary discipline to be a good ruler. For, when a ruler has learned to listen closely to the people's heart, hearing their feelings un-communicated, pains unexpressed and complaints not spoken of, only then can he hope to inspire confidence in his people. He can understand when something is wrong, and meet the true needs of the citizens[39].

The basic of any relation is listening as in listening you get the perspective of the subject; While observation is your own perspective.

Guidelines for electing political representative

Viewing those mud houses and imagining the tiresome faces of those children returning to home after the day-long labor, I miss the presence of thoughtful policies. My objective is to learn the best policy practices around the globe and take them to my land to rescue those innocent lives buried deep under economic pressure[40]. Deciding which candidate to vote into office is simply a matter of party affiliation for many people. Others, however, cast their votes based on specific

---

[39] Chinese wisdom, *English 9*, (Lahore: Punjab Text Book Board: 2011).
[40] Maria Awwal, (2017) BS student Government and Public Policy, National Defence University, Islamabad

characteristics they look for in their candidate of choice. So what are the qualities or characteristics good political leaders should possess? Here are the top 5 characteristics of some of the world's most successful political leaders[41].

- *Honesty:* Honesty develops character and builds credibility and trust, which is the foundation to evoke confidence and respect from those around you, especially in the case of political leaders, teammates and constituents.
- *Compassion:* Compassion is the humane quality of understanding the suffering of others and wanting to do something to alleviate that suffering. True compassion is a characteristic that converts knowledge to wisdom.
- *Integrity:* The word integrity is defined as 'the adherence to moral and ethical principles and the soundness of moral character.' A leader must have the trust of followers. This requires the highest standard of integrity.
- *Confidence:* Leaders who possess this quality inspire others, drawing on a level of trust which sparks the motivation to get others on board and get the job done.
- *Flexibility:* Flexibility for a political leader is about understanding the give-and-take aspects of politics, and the ability to find the common ground. This characteristic allows political leaders to recognize setbacks and criticism.

Moral: Maximize accountability in governance.

Exercise

- *Learn political thought and practices*
- *Consciously vote on elections day*
- *Scaling the political literacy:_*Ask the following qualitative questions to yourself and others

Did you acquire your CNIC in order to *cast a vote*?

---

[41] "Characteristics of good political leaders" accessed on Nov 12, 2017, http://www.beliefnet.com

Are you *registered* in the voters' list?

Do you know your *constituency* to vote in elections?

Do you take interest in *discussions or debates* about political issues?

VI. Justice thought

How can/should we appreciate justice?

Justice is about peace, and genuine respect for people. Procedural justice concerns the fairness and the transparency of the processes by which decisions are made, and may be contrasted with distributive justice (fairness in the distribution of rights or resources), and retributive justice (fairness in the punishment of wrongs). *Distributive justice* concerns the nature of a socially just allocation of goods. A society in which inequalities in outcome do not arise would be considered a society guided by the principles of a *distributive justice*. A person is known to the extent of his style of behavior to uphold *balance/justice in* social, economic, and political thoughts & practices.

Guidelines for justice

Quran says,"It is the Lord of Mercy who taught the Quran. He created man and taught him to communicate. The sun and moon follow their calculated courses; the plants and trees submit to his designs. He has raised up the sky. He has set the balance (Justice). So you may not exceed in the balance, weigh with justice and do not fall short in the balance[42]." Quran says, "Uphold justice and bear witness to God, even it is against yourselves, your parents, or your close relatives[43]."

Scaling justice: If one over-retaliates, the other person has the right to counter-retaliate. It is against religious doctrine to over-retaliate or to cross the line in getting revenge. If one slanders another he must receive the religious punishment (*hadd*) and if one wrongfully hits another he must pay blood-money (*dīyah*). For example, suppose someone slapped you and your skin became red, but when you retaliated you slapped him and his skin became black. Here, you must pay the amount

---

[42] Al-Quran, Al-Rahman, Ayat: 1-9

[43] Al-Quran, Al-Sura Nisa, Ayat: 134

of gold specified in the books of jurisprudence under the section of blood-money.

Moral: Submit witness for truth in all circumstances.

VII. Global thought

How can/should we participate in the globalization?

Globalization "is the closer integration of the countries and peoples of the world ...brought about by the enormous reduction of costs of transportation and communication, and the breaking down of artificial barriers to the flows of goods, services, capital, knowledge, and people across borders[44]." A person is known to the extent of his style of behavior to feel for humanity while thinking, wording and acting any standard of deeds.

The intensive and extensive globalization has signed thoughtless language, and thoughtless relations, through social media among the peoples. It has infected distortions in the family institution, and mental garbage across the societies. The globalized societies face threats to their eating and dressing values. The sleeping habits are perturbed as well. The nocturnal[45] has been increased in Pakistan particularly. The day sleeping has emerged a socio-economic problem because nocturnal persons are found burdening the household economy by over using food and energy resources. Particularly youth is found addicted to night wakeups without positive thoughts and practices.

Call of the day is harmony with globalization and nature. The following piece of knowledge seems 'INSPIRING. "In *Bhutan* we wear Gho. In Bhutan everyone wears Gho and like our women we men wear bright colors but unlike our women, our men get to show off their legs. Like our dress, my country's promise to remain carbon neutral is also unique. Bhutan is a small country in the Himalayas which is assumed to be a big monastery populated with happy monks. The total population is 700, 000 sand-witched between the two most populated countries the China and the India. We are a small underdeveloped country doing

---

[44] Stiglitz, Joseph E. *Globalization and its Discontents,* (New York: W.W. Norton: 2002).
[45] Nocturnal: done, occurring, or active at night.

our best to survive; in fact we are thriving. The reason we have been thriving is that we have been blessed with extra ordinary kings. Our enlightened monarchs have worked tirelessly to develop our country by balancing economic growth carefully with social development, ensuring environmental sustainability and maintaining cultural preservation, all within the *framework of good governance*. We call this holistic approach to development, 'Gross National Happiness' (GNH). In 1970s, our fourth king famously pronounced that Bhutan's Gross National Happiness is more important than Gross National Product. Ever since, all development in Bhutan is driven by GNH, a pioneering vision that aims to improve the happiness and well being of our people. But that's easier said than done, especially when you are one of the smallest economies in the world. Our entire GDP is less than two billion dollars. Our economy is small but education is completely free, all citizens are guaranteed free school education and those who work hard are given free college education. Health care is also completely free; medical consultation, medical treatment and medicines are provided by the state. We manage this because, we use our limited resources very carefully and because we stay faithful to the core mission of GNH i.e. *development with values*. Our economy is small and we must strengthen it, economic growth is important, but that economic growth must not come from undermining our unique culture or our *pristine environment*. Today our culture is flourishing, we continue to celebrate our art and architecture, food and festivals, monks and monasteries and yes we celebrate our national dress, too. This is why I can wear my Gho with pride.

Our culture is flourishing and so is our environment. 72% of my country is under forest cover. Our constitution demands that a minimum of 60% of Bhutan's total cover shall remain under forest cover for all time. Incidentally, our king used this constitution to flourish democracy he included provisions in the constitution to empower people to impeach their kings and included provisions that require all our kings to retire at the age of 65.

In a world that is threatened by climate change we are a carbon neutral country. Out of 200+ countries in the world today, we are the only carbon neutral country. Our entire country generates 2.2 million tons of carbon dioxide. Our forests sequester more than three times of that amount, so we are in a net carbon sink for more than four million tons of carbon dioxide each year. We export the renewable electricity that we generate from our fast flowing rivers. Today the clean energy that we export offsets about six million tons of carbon dioxide into the neighborhood. By 2020, we would be exporting enough electricity to offset 17 million tons of carbon dioxide. The green energy that we export would offset something like 50 million tons of carbon dioxide a year. That is more carbon dioxide than what the entire city of New York produces in one year. So inside our country we are in net carbon sink and outside we are offsetting carbon.

The world is getting warmer and climate change is a reality. My country is also being affected by climate change. Our glaciers are melting, causing flash floods and landslides, which in turn are causing disasters and widespread destruction in our country. We have 2,700 of glacial lakes which are melting day by day.

My country and my people have done nothing to contribute to global warming, but we are already bearing the brunt of its consequences and for a small country which is landlocked and mountainous, it is very difficult. *But we are not going to sit on our hands doing nothing. We will fight the climate change.* That's why we have promised to remain carbon neutral. We first made this promise in 2009 during COP15 in Copenhagen but no one noticed but in COP 21 we were heard and acknowledged by the world because the world wanted to unite and cooperate towards a solution.

We will remain faithful to our promise, Bhutan will remain carbon neutral. Here are some of the ways we are making it possible. We are providing free electricity to our farmers. The idea is that, with free electricity farmers won't use firewood to cook their food. We are investing in sustainable transport and subsidizing the purchase of electric vehicles. Similarly, we are subsidizing the costs of LED lights and our entire government is trying to go paperless. We are cleaning up our entire country through clean Bhutan, a national program. We are planting trees throughout our country, through green Bhutan, another national program. But our protected areas are at the core of our carbon neutral strategy. Our protected areas are our carbon sink, they are our lungs. Today more than half of our land is protected as national parks, nature reserves and wildlife sanctuaries. But the beauty is that we have connected them all with one another through a network of biological corridors. Now this means that our animals are free to roam throughout our country.

A tiger was spotted at 250 meters above sea level in the hot, subtropical jungle. Two years later, that same tiger was spotted near 4,000 meters in our cold alpine mountain. We should keep our parks awesome. So every year we keep aside resources to prevent poaching, hunting, mining and pollution in our parks and resources to help communities who live in those parks, manage their forests, adapt to climate change and lead better lives while continuing to live in harmony with the nature[46]."

Guidelines for the management of global thought

In foreign policy perspective 'International game entails something throwing sharpest knives at you. It depends on your skills whether you catch those by blade or handle.

For an inclusive unity, "Beyond the mountains there are people too[47]."

Iqbal says:

مشرق سے ہو بیزار، نہ مغرب سے حذر کر فطرت کا اشارہ ہے کہ شب کو سحر

Don't shun the East, nor look on West with scorn,
Since Nature yearns for change of night to morn.

Quran says, "Prophet tell believing men to lower their glances, guard their private parts: that is purer for them. God is aware of everything what they do[48]."

---

[46] Tshering Tobgay, 2016, Prime Minister of Bhutan accessed on February 26, 2018, https://www.ted.com/talks/ tshering tobgay this country isn t just carbon neutral it s carbon negative

[47] "Norwegian proverb" accessed June 2, 2018, https://www.google.com.pk

[48] Al-Quran, Al-Noor, Ayat: 30

Quran says, "Children of Adam, dress well, whenever you are at worship, and eat and drink, but do not be extravagant: Allah does not like extravagant people."[49]

Quran says, "Give you sleep for rest, the night as cover, and the day for livelihood."[50]

Exercise

- *Organize compatibility with the nature* to set your time table; with due regard to sunset and sunrise. Offer five times prayers a day.
- *Keep your gaze down*; hold on to piety and go for marriage to take the responsibility of male-female relationship.
- *Go for organic food* and indigenous cuisine
- *Choose some middle* stuff for consumption do not spend only for the name of the brand.
- *Scaling global perspectives in daily life:* Ask the following qualitative questions to yourself and others

How much you are inclined to 'Day sleeping', you start day at 9, 10 or 11 AM?

If you start at 9, you have full day. If you start at 10, you have 2/3 day. If you start at 11 you have 1/3 day. If you start after 11, then you lose the whole day.

How much you are inclined to the concept of boy friend and girl friend?

How many times in a week you eat fast food; Mcdonald or KFC?

How much you take pride in Branded garments and other products?

Moral: Think globally and act locally.

Please rise to say:

May we have the heavenly aroma of thoughts and deeds, for weaving the infrastructure of much needed contentment in a growing scary context.

---

[49] Al-Quran, Al-A raf, Ayat: 31
[50] Al-Quran, Al-Naba, Ayat: 9-11

CHAPTER 5

THOUGHTFULLY INTELLIGENT INDIVIDUALS

Now locate yourself in the system of humanity as per your *knowledge* of past, =present & future relevant to the situation. Locate yourself in the system of humanity as per your *status* relevant to you, to your family and to your community & nation. To begin with, if you want to thrive personally and professionally, and want to enjoy healthy relationships then start treating 'yourself' like you would treat someone you dearly love. How can you expect to rise higher in this life if your inner conversation is impure? Your outer world is a reflection of your inner paradigm.

I suggest you thoughtful intelligence that is the higher order of thinking to train the mind-set to produce intentions and actions. Thoughtful intelligence can be struggled for and acquired. It is comprised of capacity to understand and realize the impact of one's thoughts, words and actions on others' (individuals', groups', and nations') survival, dignity[1] and development in time (days, weeks, months or years) and space (geographical land with or without human beings). It establishes thoughtful thoughts. Per the inner paradigm[2]: Thoughtful intelligence establishes and defends moral values in the individual against internal and external threats. This defense includes detection, prevention and response to threats through the use of moral beliefs, values, rules and

---

[1] Alquran, Sura Bani Israel, Ayat: 70 'And We have certainly honored the children of Adam.'
[2] The inner paradigm is a framework containing all the accepted views of an individual about human life (past, present, and future); inclusive social, economic, political, and security dimensions.

practices. Thoughtful intelligence visions the eyes to observe and gives the courage[3] to understand befittingly suited to difficult times; and reveals compassion[4] for moral development.

Khizra's mentor Qareeb advises, "Take your time, learn how to appreciate, and then go to meet your charismatic 'Self'. For this purpose you need a thoughtful mind and a grateful heart." Chapter 5 is about self-relationship. Your evolution over earlier four chapters gives you a choice to assert yourself to protect your mind and being as precious aspects of your identity. This flagship carries the following to supersize your effort:

I. Manual to operate change
II. Spiritual self-care
III. Physical self-care
IV. Lifestyle self-care

Change is constant and it's one of the only things you can rely on! To vitalize all above 'Self-Cares' you have to operate change.

I. Manual to operate change

"Yesterday I was clever, so I wanted to change the world. Today I am wise, so I am changing myself[5]." Following are the principles of change:

Act upon your knowledge: Everything you've learned in life and read in self-help...practice it. Transformation happens in practice. Act upon the knowledge that will take you into the life you desire.

Face your challenges: Studies show that the more you postpone something, the more anxiety and tension you generate. Write short weekly lists of tasks and complete them.

Start in being proactive mode: There are two ways of operating in your daily life, and this holds true for your personal life and your professional life. The two modes are proactive and reactive. Problems

---

[3] Courage is the ability to do something that frightens one: bravery.
[4] Compassion is the ability to give and to forgive.
[5] Rumi, "Theosophy World," accessed March 3, 2018, https://www.theosophy.world/resource/quotes/quotes-rumi

arise when you live predominantly in the reactionary mode. You have to learn: how to operate in the proactive mode.

Practice the art of saying No: Stop saying yes to everyone. If you say yes to everyone and everything out of habit, you leave no space, time or energy to channel into what is the most appropriate. By practicing this habit, you might also become famous for your 'Hipocrisy'. If you are willing to **change your rationale** about how you live your life, you will find there is far more room for a shift in your experience than you might realize. Each time you stumble, pick yourself up, and practice again, and again, and again. That is the foundation of all sustainable change.

Moral: You are bigger and stronger than the challenge you face!

II. Spiritual self-care

The benchmark is connectivity regarding spiritual dynamic and its intensity. I refer here to the concepts of: purpose of life, prayer and meditation, self-compassion, positive thoughts, and mentorship to approach the objectivity of spiritual self-care.

Self assertion-Finding your purpose of life: Listen to what yours being needs and nourish it. Listen to what your intuition tells you and act upon it to find out the purpose of your life. You have to start to watch your thoughts, and to witness your feelings and notice how they impact your choices. You have to **notice your decision making process and rationale.** Once you understand that how you have been operating, with clarity. You can confidently make better choices, with new tools to exercise your courage muscle to go for self assertion. Being assertive helps to improve yours self-thought.

You can only solve a problem by assessing it, understanding it, and through bringing a ***different*** *thinking,* energy and intention to it, in comparison to the thinking that created it in the first place. You must *adopt resolving attitude* **to reach the purpose of life.** Talk about the problem by all means: but for two reasons only; firstly, to see what you can learn from it and secondly to devise a solution for it.

There comes a point in life when you have to make a choice. The choice is to greet every day with a compassionate heart, awareness, and an open mindedness. For this purpose, you have to say "YES!" to your life and "YES!" to owning your space here on this planet so that you can attain full potential and make your unique contribution towards this world. Think that what is profitable as per your capacity for the system of humanity should be known to you as your success and purpose of life.

Moral: You are unique with a unique purpose of life.

Exercise

Be assertive, ask what you want and say what you think.

Prayer and meditation: Prayer is the expression of thanks addressed to God. We have clear advice to pray to Allah. Quran says, "[O Prophet], recite that has been revealed to you of the scripture; keep up the prayer: prayer restraints outrageous and unacceptable behavior. Remembering God is greater. God knows everything you are doing[6]."

Meditation: Meditation is contemplation and thinking. Night prayer has depth because you listen as well, what you speak to your Lord. We have been advised to offer *Tahajjad.* Quran says,"And during the night wake up and pray, as an extra offering of your own, so that your Lord raise you to highly praised status[7]."

Iqbal says:

جب عشق سکھاتا ہے آداب خود آگاہی کھلتے ہیں اس غلاموں پر اسرار شہنشاہی
عطار ہو، رومی ہو، رازی ہو، غزالی ہو کچھ ہاتھ نہیں آتا بے آہ سحر گاہی
When man grows self- awareness, he learns the kingly deeds. Like Rumi, Attar, Ghazzali and Razi, none can achieve the objective without the help of the morning sighs[8].

[6] Al-Quran, Al-Ankabut, Ayat:45
[7] Al-Quran, Al-Isra, Ayat:79
[8] Muhammad. Iqbal, accessed Sep 2, 2017, https://www.iap.gov.pk/

Iqbal says:

ہوا میں گرچہ تھی شمشیر کی تیزی نہ چھوٹے لندن میں بھی مجھ سے آدابِ سحر خیزی

Though at London, winter wind was sharp like sword,
but my rise at early morning didn't miss out[9].

Exercise

Offer five times prayer daily and Tahajjud at least once in a week on every Friday.

Self-compassion: Compassion is sympathetic pity and concern for the sufferings or misfortunes of others. Self should be treated with compassion as well with the application of self forgiveness, self helping, positive self talk, and friendship with yourself. "Self-compassion involves treating yourself with the same kindness, concern, and support you'd show to a good friend. When faced with difficult life struggle, or confronting personal mistakes, failures, and inadequacies. Self-compassion responds with kindness rather than harsh self-judgment, recognizing that imperfection is part of the shared human experience."[10] To become more self-compassionate, try the following 7 steps:

1. Recognize that you are experiencing self-distress: adopt an attitude in which you deliberately pay attention to your inner experience so that you can notice when you began to shift into a negative state.

2. Accept that the feeling is there: make a conscious decision to sit with whatever negative feeling is there and try to accept it.

3. Imagine what you might feel if you saw a loved one experiencing this feeling: in your mind's eye, imagine your loved ones being scared or sad or feeling bad about themselves. Then think about what you might feel. Perhaps you would feel the urge to help or comfort them. Try to direct this compassionate mind-set towards yourself. If you notice any resistance or thoughts of "I don't deserve compassion," acknowledge them, and try to direct compassion to yourself anyway.

---

[9] Muhammad. Iqbal, accessed Sep 2, 2017, https://www.iap.gov.pk/
[10] "Self-Compassion: What It Is, What It Does, and How It Relates to Mindfulness," accessed Sep 28, 2018, *http://citeseerx.ist.psu.edu/viewdoc/* Kristin D. Neff, Katie A. Dahm, B. Meier

4. Challenge your negative story about yourself: the ways to challenge the story are to ask yourself if you're being too judgmental, or if you're seeing the situation from only one perspective. Are there any other, kinder ways to view the situation? Are you expecting yourself to be without mistake?

5. Think about how everybody messes up sometimes: In fact, even the most successful people make serious mistakes. Think about all the mistakes politicians make. But making a mistake doesn't undo all of your accomplishments and successes. Neff[11] cites "common humanity" as an aspect of self-compassion: Humans are learning, developing beings rather than finished products. We're all works in progress.

6. Decide what it would take to *forgive* yourself: if your behavior hurt you or another person, ask yourself what it would take to forgive yourself. Think about whether you want to apologize and make amends to the person you hurt. If you hurt *yourself* through addictive behavior, avoidance, ruining relationships, or otherwise behaving unwisely, make a coping plan for the next time you are in a similar situation so that you can begin to act differently.

7. Use self-talk to encourage yourself: you may say something like, "It doesn't help to beat yourself up," or, "Everybody makes mistakes sometimes." You may want to acknowledge yourself for trying, even if you weren't successful. You may tell yourself to focus on the positive aspects of what you did as well as the negative ones, or that behavior change is a process, and you need to keep trying.

Exercise

Learn to celebrate failure.

Cultivate positive thoughts: Please follow the chapter 4 of this book.

Find Mentorship: Mentorship is the guidance provided by a mentor, especially an experienced person in a company or an educational institution. The benchmark is connectivity with a thoughtful community and the intensity of the same. Here I refer to three groups in order to find mentorship; family, friends and teachers.

---

[11] Ibid

III. Physical self-care

Always prioritize wellness because Physical health is critical for the overall well-being. It is the most visible of the various dimensions of health including social, intellectual, emotional, and the spiritual health. Some of the most obvious and serious indications of our unhealthiness appear physically. I refer the following for physical self-care.

Regular activity: should be maintained as the only way for physical self-care.

a. Practice physical activity helps to improve mood. Spending 40 minutes in walk/exercise every day is the best antidote against sadness and stress.
b. Take care of your posture. Walk straight with your shoulders slightly backwards. The front view helps to maintain a good mood.
c. Practice swimming if you get the opportunity
d. Practice horse riding. Our Prophet Muhammad (PBUH) was a very good horse rider, and Prophet Soleman had great liking for the horses.

Dietary patterns: One will be healthy if he follows the middle course regarding the desire for food. The middle course in eating means eating the necessary amount and variety of food. The Qurān orders, *"Eat and drink, but do not be excessive[12]."* The Prophet Muhammad (PBUH) advises, *"One should not eat until one is hungry and should stop eating before one is full[13]."* The poet Sʿadī has wrote a poem in this regards: *"Do not eat so much so that food falls out of your mouth and do not eat so little so that you die of weakness[14]."* Never become accustomed to eating all kinds of different food at once. The more kinds of food that man eats the more health problems he will have.

One who is used to eating different kind of foods will also spend a lot of money. For this reason it is possible for him to commit any crime in

---

[12] Islamic Ethics, accessed on Oct 31, 2017, https://www.al-islam.org
[13] Ibid
[14] Ibid

order to provide his stomach with what it wants. But when one is satisfied with whatever is brought to him, and does not care to eat different kinds of food then he will not commit these crimes; instead he will fight against his '*nafs*'. Abu Dharr fought against his personal desires and did not accept Mu'āwīyah's elaborate dinner invitations or pouches of gold. Instead, he was satisfied with barley bread. One who is satisfied is honored. He pays attention to what is allowed and what is forbidden.

Exercise

a. Drink eight glasses of water daily. Learn from Quran, "We made every living thing from water[15]."

b. Eat all things advised Halal by Prophet Muhammad (PBUH) available in relevant seasons and geographical areas.

c. Have Breakfast. Some people miss breakfast due to the lack of time or not to get fat. Studies show that breakfast gives you energy, helps you think and perform your activities successfully.

d. What you eat has an impact on your mood - Do not skip meals, eat lightly every 3 to 4 hours and keep glucose levels stable. Avoid excessive white flour and sugar. Eat everything but eat healthy.

e. Plan your diet that if you may get delicious healthy food then it should contain all the necessary medicinal and nutritional values.

f. Do not eat in reclining position or when lying prone on one's stomach

g. When it is time for prayer and the food is being served, eat first and then pray

h. Wash your hands before and after a meal

i. Mention Allah's name before eating or drinking and praise Allah afterwards

j. Eat with the right hand.

k. Eat from what is next or nearest to you.

l. Eat from the sides of a dish, and not from its middle or upper top

m. Do not find fault with the food.

n. While drinking, pause three times in order to breathe.

---

[15] Al-Quran, Al-Anbiya, Ayat:30

Bathroom and rest room manners: One of the least discussed etiquette topics is bathroom etiquette, but it's the one that needs to be addressed. Whether you need to use the bathroom while visiting a friend or you're using a public restroom, follow these guidelines for good restroom manners.

- Close the door, avoid chatter, ignore cell phone, flush the toilet and cover the evidence, dispose of personal hygiene products, wash your hands.
- Leave the restroom or bathroom in as good of condition as you found it or you desire to find. This means that men should check the floor around the toilet and wipe up splatters.
- Say Alhamdulillah after sneezing, and try to keep the sound of sneeze as low as possible.

Take adequate sleep: Adequate sleep is a key part of a healthy lifestyle, and can benefit your heart, weight, mind, skin and more. A person should get 6-7 hours of daily sleep. The ritual of getting a proper *sleep is being* ignored these days due to today's materialistic lifestyle. Quran advises, "We made the night as cover, and the day for your livelihood[16]."

Exercise
- Before going to sleep, close and lock the doors and extinguish the fire lamp
- Dusting off the bed before lying down on it
- Sleep on your right side and place your cheek on your right hand
- Recite something from the Quran

Weekly beauty care: We are advised by Prophet Muhammad (PBUH) to have thorough cleaning and cleansing of body on every Friday by trimming nails as well.

Exercise
Give yourself scalp massage at least once a week for 10 minutes to increase blood flow to the scalp and promote hair growth. Skin should

---

[16] Al-Quran, Al-Naba, Ayat:10-11

be cared through scrubbing and toning. They are important to balance excessive oil, refining pores and providing nourishment to skin.

IV. Lifestyle self-care

Here I refer to the dynamic life balance among self, nature, and society.

Regular routines and structures: Regular routines and structures depend on the punctuality component of the individual. Punctuality does not mean only to organize your daily tasks around the 24 hours clock, but it also means:

a. That you punctuate your thoughts with the belief in oneness of Allah and Prophet Muhammad (PBUH) as his last messenger.
b. That you punctuate your thoughts to righteousness
c. That you punctuate your deeds to have compatibility with nature, and seasons
d. That you punctuate your rights to duties
e. That you punctuate your vision to create profitability in the system of humanity
f. That you punctuate your deeds to facilitate the others
g. That you punctuate your deeds by counting their impact on the life hereafter

Book reading: Reading requires one to identify and understand strings of words in a fluid manner. It is a detailed process that includes comprehension, word recognition, engagement, and fluency.

Exercise

•   Read the translation of Quran and learn Hadith. Read the governance system of Madina established by Prophet Muhammad (PBUH) and followed by four Caliphs of Islam.
•   Indulge into literature, history and biographies of heros like, Quaid-e-Azam, Allama Iqbal, Abraham Lincoln and Nelson Mandela.

76

Take time in nature: Spending time in nature isn't just a "nice to have activity," but it's actually really important for your optimal health. The sounds of nature shift your nervous system into a relaxed state. Being closer to the nature is associated with healthier blood pressure levels.

In Quran, nature is presented as the precise gift of the Lord. "With shading branches' which, then, of your Lord's blessing do you both deny? With a pair of flowing springs which, then, of your Lord's blessing do you both deny[17]?"

Travelling: Travel is the movement of people between relatively distant geographical locations, and can involve *travel* by foot, bicycle, automobile, train, boat, bus, airplane, or other means, with or without luggage, and can be one way or round trip. The Prophet Muhammad (PBUH) has admired travelling. He advised to travel to obtain knowledge even if you have to go to China[18].

Exercise

- Bid farewell to wife, relatives and friends before commencing the journey.
- Start your travel at the beginning of the day.
- Supplicate that are relevant to travel.

Dressing: A thoughtfully intelligent person dresses decently to provide a decent outlook. He/she reflects wisdom with a combination of his/her sensible social role, by decently covering the body and the body contours. Decent dressing is the Universal value; therefore decent dressing should be promoted to format civilized identity and dignity. Prophet Muhammad (PBUH) says, "If Allah blesses one with wealth, the effects of that blessing should be seen in his clothes[19]."

Decent sense of dressing surrounds the following thoughts:

1. Assigned role (student/teacher/manager)
2. Social role (Daughter/Son, Mother/Father)

[17] Al-Quran, Al-Rehman, Ayat:48-51
[18] "Seek Knowledge Even If You Have To Go To China.", accessed January 3, 2018, http://www.al-mawrid.org
[19] Islamic Ethics, accessed on Oct 31, 2017, https://www.al-islam.org

3. Weather situation (summer/winter)
4. Impact on others glancing at the wearer
5. No negative dressing[20]
6. Dupatta (Pakistani scarf) is mandatory in women wear. At the very least it must be hanging on the shoulders.
7. Wear comfortable shoes because if your feet hurt you will become moody, says Dr. KeinthWapner[21].

Exercise

*   Do not drag your garment on the ground with a feeling of haughtiness and self-conceit
*   Do not wear extravagant clothes to gain fame or to draw the attention of others
*   Wear fragrance
*   Man should not wear lethargy beard, he should refine his beard

Comedy: Comedy is a play characterized by its humorous or satirical tone and its depiction of amusing people or incidents, in which the characters ultimately triumph over adversity[22].

Exercise

*   Read comedy
*   Watch comedy of Moeen Akhtar and Anwar Maqsood[23].

Music: Listen to music. It is proven that listening to music awakens you to but the words and rhymes in music should contain effective poetry following the morals.

---

[20] Negative dressing includes skin tights, see through outfits and sleeveless shirts.

[21] "Orthopedic Surgery" accessed Sep 28, 2018, https://health.usnews.com/doctors/keith-wapner

[22] "Shakespeare's comedies" Bloom, Harold. William Shakespeare: The Comedies. Blooms Critical Views, 2009.

[23] Moin Akhtar, was a Pakistani television, film, stage actor, humorist, comedian, impersonator, and a host, writer, singer, director and producer who rose to fame in era of Radio Pakistan along with his co-actors Anwer Maqsood and Bushra Ansari.

Exercise

- Listen to the music which takes you near to the Lord.

Moral: Inner 'Goodness' glows the 'Exterior' of the individual and radiates his thoughtful aura in the society.

Please rise to say:

My longing comes to my lips as supplication of mine
O God! May like the candle be the life of mine!

May the world's darkness disappear through the life of mine!
May every place light up with the sparkling light of mine!

May my homeland through me attain elegance
As the garden through flowers attains elegance

May my life like that of the moth be, O Lord!
May I love the lamp of knowledge, O Lord!

May supportive of the poor my life's way be
May loving the old, the suffering my way be

O God! Protect me from the evil ways
Show me the path leading to the good ways[24]

---

[24] Muhammad. Iqbal, accessed Sep 2, 2017, https://www.iap.gov.pk/

CHAPTER 6

THOUGHTFULLY INTELLIGENT INDIVIDUALS AND INFORMAL MORAL DEVELOPMENT

Thoughtful models and practices raft moral development. Maryam[1] studies in BS program at National Defence University Islamabad. A student requested to use her USB as he greatly needed it for his presentation at that moment in the class. She was generous enough to lend him. Instead of returning the USB, he forwarded it to someone else. When the next day Mariam asked for USB; he took it very lightly and expressed the negative notion that Mariam was too careful about her belongings. Similarly Mariam's friend Mona who used to bring safe water to drink in a bottle-- lost her bottle. A fellow asked her for a sip in the class but did not return the bottle. The moment she inquired about her bottle, the other started taunting her about her miserly nature. Such dispositions indicate the *initial levels of moral depravity*; in first example Mariam is excellent to help the other in need but the other person's act of not returning the USB tells the *betrayal of agreement*; the second example indicates the *exploitation of free facility*. Thoughtful intelligence is about knowing what to do when there are no rules.

Thoughtful intelligence is the higher order of thinking to train the mind-set to produces intentions and actions. Thoughtful intelligence can be struggled for and acquired. It is comprised of capacity to understand and realize the impact of one's thoughts, words and actions on others'

---

[1] Maryam is found a different student in behavior as compared to others because of her *generosity*. She shares her knowledge and belongings with other students.

(individuals', groups', and nations') survival, dignity[2] and development in time (days, weeks, months or years) and space (geographical land with or without human beings). It establishes thoughtful thoughts. Per the inner paradigm[3]: Thoughtful intelligence establishes and defends moral values in the individual against internal and external threats. This defense includes detection, prevention and response to threats through the use of moral beliefs, values, rules and practices. Thoughtful intelligence visions the eyes to observe and gives the courage[4] to understand befittingly suited to difficult times; and reveals compassion[5] for moral development.

Khizra's mentor Qareeb says, "Let them accuse you of being 'Righteous', meanwhile hold the sharp knife of inner cleansing based on thoughtful thoughts and chip out 'Secretly' your opponents." Chapters 2, 3, 4, and 5 propounded the life of a thoughtful individual. Now chapter 6 deals with the plan to initiate and expand thoughtfully intelligent community. I dare to prompt the following:

I. Concept of informal moral development
II. The greatest mutuality
III. Mutuality with the Creator
IV. Mutuality with the humanity
V. Threats to mutuality with the humanity
VI. Mutuality with the nature

I. Concept of informal moral development

I am humbled to Allah for giving the following knowledge to establish the framework of informal moral development:

"It is the Lord of Mercy, who taught the Quran, he created man, and taught him to communicate, the sun and moon follow their calculated

---

[2] Al-Quran, Bani Israel, Ayat: 70 'And We have certainly honored the children of Adam'
[3] The inner paradigm is a framework containing all the accepted views of an individual about human life (past, present, and future); inclusive social, economic, political, and security dimensions.
[4] Courage is the ability to do something that frightens one: bravery.
[5] Compassion is the ability to give and to forgive.

courses, the plants and the trees submit to his designs, he has raised up the sky, he has set the balance[6]."

The verses maximize the perception of 'Punctuality' as the universal moral. Punctuality does not mean only to organize your routine tasks around a 24 hours clock, but it means:

1. That you punctuate your thoughts with the belief in <u>oneness</u> of Allah and Prophet Muhammad (PBUH) as his last messenger.
2. That you punctuate your thoughts to <u>righteousness</u>
3. That you punctuate your deeds to have <u>compatibility with nature</u>, and seasons
4. That you punctuate your rights to <u>duties</u>
5. That you punctuate your vision to create <u>profitability in the system of humanity</u>
6. That you punctuate your deeds to <u>facilitate the others</u>
7. That you punctuate your deeds by counting their impact on the <u>life hereafter</u>

There are four hormones which determine a human's happiness - Endorphins, Dopamine, Serotonin, and Oxytocin. It is important that we understand these hormones, as we need all four of them to stay happy.

1. Endorphins. When we exercise, the body releases Endorphins. This hormone helps the body cope with the pain of exercising. We then enjoy exercising because these Endorphins will make us happy. Laughter is another good way of generating Endorphins. We need to spend 30 minutes exercising every day, read or watch funny stuff to get our day's dose of Endorphins.
2. Dopamine. In our journey of life, we accomplish many little and big tasks, it releases various levels of Dopamine. When we get appreciated for our work at the office or at home, we feel accomplished and good, that is because it releases Dopamine. This also explains why most housewives are unhappy since they rarely get acknowledged or appreciated for their work.

---

[6] Al-Quran, Al-Rehman, Ayat:1-7

3. Serotonin is released when we act in a way that benefits others. When we transcend ourselves and give back to others or to nature or to the society, it releases Serotonin. Even, providing useful information on the internet like writing information blogs, answering people's questions will generate Serotonin. That is because we will use our precious time to help other people via our answers or articles.

4. Oxytocin: It is released when we become close to other human beings. When we hug our friends or family, Oxytocin is released. Similarly, when we shake hands or put our arms around someone's shoulders, various amounts of Oxytocin are released.

So, it is simple, we must exercise every day to get Endorphins, we must accomplish little goals and get Dopamine, we need to be nice to others to get Serotonin and finally hug our kids, friends, and families to get Oxytocin and we will be happy. When we are happy, we can deal with our challenges and problems better. I assume that following notions of the chapter 6 will help the above mentioned hormones.

II. The greatest mutuality

Mutuality is sharing of a thought feeling, action, or a relationship between two or more entities. The very notion of punctuality (as above seven points) causes greatest mutuality referred to a human being with the Creator, humanity and the nature (see Figure 1).

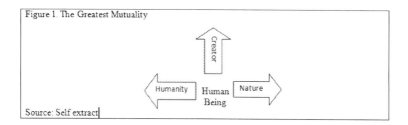

Figure 1. The Greatest Mutuality

Source: Self extract

The thoughtfully intelligent individual celebrates the dignity of all times (past-present-future) because of connectivity with the Creator, Humanity and Nature.

III. Mutuality with the Creator

All the human beings are unique in biological and thinking traits. This fact moves us to believe that the God is unique who has created so many unique human beings. Quran says, "Say, 'He is God the One, God the eternal, He begot no one nor was he begotten, No one is comparable to Him[7]."

Iqbal says:

خودی کا سر نہاں لا الہ الا اللہ
خودی ہے تیغِ فساں لا الہ الا اللہ

The secret of the Self is hid, In words "No God but Allah alone".
The Self is just a dull-edged sword, "No
God but He", the grinding stone[8].

Prophet Muhammad is the last messenger of Allah and he is found the BEST in character. Quran says, "Truly you (MUHAMMAD) have strong character[9]." To earn closeness to Lord the individual should have enough thoughts to pray (I covered it in chapter 4-5); here I highlight supplication.

Iqbal says:

کی محمدؐ سے فا تو نے تو ہم تیرے ہیں
یہ جہاں چیز ہے کیا لوح و قلم تیرے ہیں

If you are loyal to Muhammad PBUH we are yours;
This universe is nothing the Tablet and the
Pen are yours to write destiny[10].

---

[7] Al, Quran, Al-Ikhlas, Ayat:1-4
[8] I Muhammad. Iqbal, accessed Sep 2, 2017, https://www.iap.gov.pk/
[9] Al, Quran, Al-Qalam, Ayat:4
[10] Muhammad. Iqbal, accessed Sep 2, 2017, https://www.iap.gov.pk/

Manners of supplication: Ultimate safety and success hinge upon one's realization of At-Tawheed- Islamic monotheism and one of the ways of realizing At-Tawheed in one's life is to supplicate to Allah only. Supplication is worship and worship is for Allah alone. There are many virtues and benefits of supplication. First, when you supplicate to Allah you will taste the spiritual sweetness of invoking Allah of humbling yourself before him breaking down before Allah and invoking Him for your needs – accompanying these is a spiritual delight that cannot be described.

Guidelines to get supplication answered

1. Duty towards one's parents is one of the ways that lead to one's supplications being answered.
2. Performing good deeds prior to supplication.
3. Performing voluntary acts of worship after obligatory ones is one of the causes that lead to a person's supplication being answered.
4. It is recommended to face the Qiblah while supplicating one must supplicate in secret, supplicate persistently and repeatedly, and ask with determination and resolve.
5. Eating from unlawfully derived wealth prevents one's supplications from being answered.

Exercise

How much you are thoughtfully intelligent in perspective of closeness to Lord?

Find out how many of the following you do or are inclined to do. If you are able to do maximum out of the following 21deeds (three uttered by each of the following 7 sources), then you have maximum thoughtful intelligence.

The most liked three things by:

1. The Prophet Muhammad (PBUH)
2. Abu Bakr As-Siddiq (Ra)
3. Umar ibn Al-Khattab (Ra)
4. Uthman ibn Affan (Ra)

5. Ali ibn Abi Talib (Ra)
6. Jibreel (As)
7. Allah The Lord of Honor

The Companions were sitting with Prophet Muhammad (PBUH).

<u>Prophet Muhammad (PBUH)</u> said, "in this world, women and perfume have been made dear to me, and the coolness of my eyes is in prayer."[11]

Perfume: The Prophet (PBUH) used to smell so good that people used to make perfume out of his sweat because it would become the most fragrant perfume.

Women: The status of women that is in Islam is unmatched compared to that in any religion or system. The status and rights of a woman in all her roles have been highly dignified.

Prayer: During 10th Hijri, the saddest year of the Prophet's life (PBUH). The love of his life Hazrat Khadeejatul-Kubra (Ra) passed away; and then his uncle. It was right in those times of pain, that Allah took him on the journey of Isra and Miraj and gave him (PBUH) the gift of prayer. Allah blessed the Prophet (PBUH), and by his extension the entire humanity, with a direct source of asking Him. This was the gift Allah gave him (PBUH) amid the year of sorrow. This was the gift Allah made the coolness of his eyes.

<u>Abu Bakr As-Siddiq</u> (Ra) said, «You have spoken the truth, O Messenger of Allah! I was made to love three things from this world – looking at the face of the Messenger of Allah, spending my wealth for the Messenger of Allah, and giving my daughter in marriage to the Messenger of Allah.»

Umar ibn Al-Khattab reported, The Messenger of Allah, peace and blessings be upon him, ordered us to give charity and at the time I possessed some wealth. I said to myself, "Today I will outdo Abu Bakr, if ever there were a day to outdo him." I went with half of my wealth to the Prophet and he said, "What have you left for your family?" I said, "The same amount." Then, Abu Bakr came with everything he had. The

---

[11] "The three things dear to Prophet Muhammad (PBUH)," accessed on Oct 31, 2017, https://www.islamweb.net/en/article/156581/the-concept-of-true-love-in-islam

Prophet said, "O Abu Bakr, what have you left for your family?" Abu Bakr said, "Allah and his messenger's name." I said, "By Allah, I will never do better than Abu Bakr."

Umar ibn Al-Khattab (Ra) said: "You have spoken truthfully, O Abu Bakr! I was made to love three things from this world – commanding good, forbidding evil, and worn garments."

"Simple and frugal; doing his duty without fear and favor; energetic even to harshness, yet capable of tenderness towards the weak; a severe judge of others and especially of himself, he was born a ruler and every inch a man[12]." On the way to Damascus (after it was liberated by Muslims in his caliphate), Hazrat Umar (Ra) and his servant were taking turns riding their horse. When they reached the city it was servant's turn to ride but he refused because he didn't want the Caliph to have his servant riding the horse when they were entering the city. Hazrat Umar said that it was unfair that he would take his servant's turn and that "the honor of Islam (i.e., being Muslim) is enough for all of us." Also, his servant asked him to change his clothes and wear an elegant robe before entering the city. He pondered the request but then decided to remain in his worn clothing. When people saw that this simple man entering the city in his patched clothes with his servant on his horse was the leader of the Muslims, they immediately accepted him as their caliph.

Uthman ibn Affan (Ra) said:" You have spoken truthfully, O Umar! And I was made to love three things from this world – feeding the hungry, clothing the naked, and reading the Qur'an."

Hazrat Uthman was known as "Ghani" — the generous. He was the exceptional exemplar of aiding the needy. In Battle of Tabuk where the Muslims were 30 thousand, he had paid for the preparation of about a third of the army. He would spend his nights in the prayer reading large portions of the Qur'an and sometimes even reading the entire Quran in one go inside the prayer.

Ali ibn Abi Talib (Ra) said: "You have spoken truthfully, O Uthman! I was made to love three things from this world – serving the guest, fasting in summer, and fighting [in the way of Allah] with the sword."

He used to fast in the hottest days of the summer of Arabia. Once when the time of Iftar finally arrived, a homeless knocked on his door

---

[12] Sheikh. Mohammad Iqbal, *The mission of Islam* (Lahore, Taj Company: 1977)

and asked for food. He instantly went back and picked up his entire Iftar and gave it to him and left nothing for himself. His entire family and the servant seeing him did the same. No one ate that evening.

Jibreel (as) also descended and when Prophet (PBUH) asked what three things would he have loved, he replied:" To guide those led astray, to keep the company of contented strangers, and to help families afflicted with hardship."

Jibreel (as) continued: "The Lord of Honor [also has now expressed that He] loves three things from His servants – giving one's utmost, crying out of regret when repenting, and being patient in times of poverty."

Giving one's utmost means that He loves the person who dedicates his most special of abilities for Him. Next, Allah himself says in the Qur'an,"Surely Allah loves those who are most repentant[13]."

And finally, Allah tells about His love and reward for As-Saabireen (the patient ones) and stresses upon the importance of Sabr (Patience) at many places in incredibly beautiful verses two of which are below. "And Allah loves the patient[14]." "Be patient, indeed the (best) outcome is for the righteous[15]."

IV. Mutuality with the humanity

Humanity is the entire human race or the characteristics that belong uniquely to human beings, such as kindness, mercy and sympathy. Humanity is all the people in the world. Humanity is treating someone with kindness. Value of Humanity is to respect the rights of every individual, and to understand and accept our own value and cherish our own right to life. Humanity is to protect the intrinsic value and potential of every individual, making no discrimination. Everyone should be able to live with respect from others.

---

[13] Al-Quran Al-Baqara, Ayat: 222
[14] Al-Quran Al-Imran, Ayat:146
[15] Al-Quran Al-Hud, Ayat:49

Iqbal says:

آدمیت احترام آدمی   باخبر شو از مقام ِ آدمی
Humanity means respect of the mankind-learn to appreciate the true worth of man[16].

Positive thinking: Find good things in others. To become motivated one needs to feel appreciated, trusted, and accepted. Not to be needed is slow death for a man. It is recognized that his power and competence were meaningless without someone to serve. Empathy, understanding, validation and compassion go a long way to assist a man in becoming more receptive and appreciative of his support. Everyone needs one time to learn how to receive while the other time needs to learn how to give. In this section I highlight the manners appreciated by human civilizations to live in a community.

Manners of greetings of peace: The thoughtful individual initiates greetings of peace. It is Sunnah to initiate greetings of peace. It is Waajib (Compulsory) to return the greetings. Manners of seeking permission to enter another person's home, room: the Sunnah is to greet first and then ask for permission to enter. The person who is seeking permission should stand to the right or to the left of the door, but not directly in front of it. Manners of meeting another person: It is recommended to shake the other person's hand. Stand to greet the other to show your honor.

Manners of being host or guest: Our prophet (PBUH) has advised to answer and accept an invitation. Serve from elder to younger and from right to left. When your guest wants to leave, it is recommended for you to accompany him to the door of your house.

Manners of gatherings: An individual should approach the gathering which takes him near to the creator and humanity. When three people are together, two should not speak secretly to the exclusion of the third. It is forbidden to listen in on other people's conversation. It is disliked to belching in the presence of others.

Manners of speech: Words have greater impact than one might think. Speak good words or remain silent. Good speech is charity. Obscene and foul language should not be used. Speak slowly, deliberately, and

---

[16] Muhammad. Iqbal, accessed Sep 2, 2017, https://www.iap.gov.pk/

succinctly. The art of conversing can be enhanced with the content of thoughtful intelligence. As usual it is comprised of certain principles such as; put others at ease, put yourself at ease, weave in all parties, establish shared interests, and actively pursue your own[17]. (See Table 6. 1, The art of conversing)

Table 6. 1 The art of conversing
Here are a few things you can do to participate in or make a conversation.
Listen and ask: Listening is as much an art as talking is. Listening means you are focusing on the subject being discussed and thinking about it in the hope that you will respond with a profound observation. If you find yourself in a conversation where one individual is taking the lead. Then the best way is to quietly listen to what s(he) has to say and reflect upon the subject matter. Think of at least one good question to ask the speaker. This will also encourage others in the group to ask questions, greatly dissolving one person's lead and giving each member an equal share in the conversation.
Body language: Body language is not only about keeping your shoulders broad and relaxed, keeping your hands out of the pockets and using an appropriate pitch of voice, but it is also about exuding confidence.
Speak eloquently: The tone and pitch of your voice plays an important role during conversations. Whispering or screech will only manifest your timidity and insecurity. Try to maintain an even tone and volume when you are presenting negating opinions so that it shows your composure and self assurance. When you speak, use correct pronunciation (e-g, Wenz-day not Wed-ness-day, peet-za not pi-za). Many people are conscious about using difficult vocabulary, just to sound intelligent during a conversation. Don't do that! If you know good stock-word, then go ahead—but if you do not, then don't fake it. It will be very apparent.
Source: Daily DAWN, July 3, 2016

---

[17] Catherine. Blyth, *In* The Art of Conversation: A Guided Tour of a Neglected Pleasure, (New York, Avery:2008).

Manners of the pathway: Lowering the gaze is equally intended for men and women. Returning greetings of peace is compulsory for the pathway and for all the situations. Removing anything that is harmful from the road or pathway is good deed. Guiding a person who is lost, helping a person climb his mount and raising his things up to him are good deeds.

Etiquettes of attending the mosque: One should not eat raw garlic, onion or anything foul before entering into mosque. Try to reach masjid early and enter with serenity.

Manners of visiting the sick: The sick should be visited as our Prophet Muhammad (PBUH) says, "whoever visits a sick person continues to remain in Khurfat of Paradise until he returns[18]." The visit to the sick should be short and comforting words should be delivered.

Manners about good neighborhood: The next door neighbor has rights over the other neighbor. The neighbor should be honored. His being and belongings must be honored. Prophet Muhammad (PBUH) says, "A Muslim is he from whose tongue and hand other Muslims are safe....[19]"

Manners of true brotherhood: In order to create a true brotherhood, one must be sincere and provide sincere advice. There should be a mutual cooperation among brothers. Humbleness and not pride should be the application of relationship. Have a heart that is free from rancor, grudge, and enmity as this is from the Prophet Muhammad's (PBUH) supplication, "And remove the rancor of my heart[20]." Have good thoughts about your brothers and do not spy. Do not call people by nicknames that are hurtful. Keep the secret of your brother and do not spread it.

Manners of interacting with one's wife: The following verse provides the framework for how a man should treat his wife. Quran says, "And they (women) have rights (over their husbands as regards living expenses) similar (to those of their husbands) over them (as regards obedience and respect) to what is reasonable[21]." Our Prophet Muhammad (PBUH) advises to treat women with gentleness and kindness.

---

[18] "The Book of Virtue and Good Manners." accessed March 12, 2018, https://www.thereligionofpeace.com

[19] 'Islam and Peace for All', accessed September 2, 2018 https://www.asicsa.co.za

[20] "And remove the rancor of my heart," accessed on Oct 31, 2017, https://www.islamweb.net/en/article/156581/the-concept-of-true-love-in-islam

[21] Al- Quran, Al-Baqra, Ayat:228

Moral: To understand someone, do not look at what he has achieved rather ponder at what he aspires to achieve.

Exercise

- Causing harm info should not be carried on. Once upon a time Sheikh Saadi experienced a man telling him that a person was abusing you in the down town. Saadi took a sigh and responded, "Dear that person was aiming the arrows in air-----you caught and brought them to hit me."
- Complain about food should be reported in beginning at restaurant. I noticed few students ate half of the meal ------ then to evade the bill complained that the food was not good.
- Praise the meal in front of others but criticize in isolation when it is prepared by sister, mother, wife or family friend.
- Cancel the reservation/booking if you are not dinning or travelling to avail the reservation so that the other person may get a chance.
- Save water and energy for the people in want of water and energy.
- Give the household budget to wife; as she knows better to run the home economy.
- Choose the right leader and do not sleep on polling day.
- Offer the honest witness services of an event in order to help justice
- Tolerate the difference of culture, identity, and opinion

V. Threats to mutuality with humanity

The following threats to mutuality with humanity must be avoided.

Hypocrisy: "A two-faced person is regarded as evil because he is like a hypocrite. He sweetly talks with falsehood and lies, and he sows dissension among people. A two faced person is the one who goes to each group with what pleases it, giving the appearance that he is from it and opposes its counterpart (or enemy). His action is pure hypocrisy, lying, deception, and trickery----But if a person goes to two groups in order to make peace between them, then he is doing something that is praiseworthy. The two-faced person praises the group he is with and finds fault with the other group. On the other hand, the praiseworthy person goes to each of the two groups with words of reconciliation, finding excuses for one group while he is with other trying to convey good points of the other group while hiding their faults[22]."

Backbiting and Slander: Prophet Muhammad (PBUH) defined backbiting, "to mention your brother with something that he dislikes." Someone asked "Suppose what I say about brother is true?" The messenger of Allah answered, "If what you said about him is true, then you have backbitten him; and if what you have said about him is false, then you have slandered him."

Better you slept: "As a young child the renowned Shaykh Saadi rahmatullahi alayh had the opportunity to perform Itikaaf with his father. At Tahajjud time father and son awoke, offered the Salaah of Tahajjud and made dua. After completing their worship Shaykh Saadi said to his father, 'These other people are so negligent that they are sleeping and not performing tahajjud.'

To this his father replied 'Saadi, it would have been better had you slept the whole night than performed tahjjud.' As Shaykh Saadi was young, he did not understand that Tahajjud was Nafl and backbiting was haram. Thus he did not appreciate that his comment had negated the benefit he had acquired by offering Tahajjud. The Shaykh's father however understood this and took the opportunity to teach his young son this important principle[23]."

VI. Mutuality with the nature

Nature is phenomena of the physical world collectively: including plants, animals, the landscape, and other features and products of the earth, as opposed to humans or human creations. Mutuality with nature goes to learn from nature and appreciation of nature.

Learn from nature: the following we learn from nature.

[22] "Hypocrisy and Islam," accessed on Oct 31, 2017, https://www.islamweb.net/en/article/156581/the-concept-of-true-love-in-islam.
[23] "Backbiting," accessed March 10, 2018, https://www.ummah.com

1) Discipline: The structural discipline practiced by sun and the moon.
2) Generosity: Each source of nature is generous e-g, sun, moon and sea----serving us all and getting nothing in return. Nature is from generosity (the creator) and is generous.
3) Precision: Each excerpt of nature is precise e-g, each leaf you ever notice is precise----so is every creation.
4) Justice: Each action of nature distributes as per the climate and weather patterns.
5) Sacrifice: Plants bear the sun to comfort us.
6) Beauty: Nature is the ultimate evidence of beauty.
7) Uniqueness: The nature is found unique----no one has ever created the piece of art like nature.

Exercise

Find out how many of above you do or you are inclined to do------If you are able to do maximum things out of 7 then you have the maximum thoughtful intelligence.

Appreciate nature: Once upon a time, a lady from Kashmir was our neighbor in Quetta. In the month of December on first snow fall of winter she sent us a tray full of fresh snow covered with Kashmiri embroidered clothe. The act was really an appreciation of winter arrival to celebrate connectivity with nature. It was also a source of celebrating connectivity with human beings. Above all, it was without any material cast. All of this indicates the sense to appreciate nature. Spend time with nature; it magnifies your being.

Iqbal says:

فطرت کے مقاصد کی کرتا ہے نگہبانی   یا بندہ صحرائی یا مردِ کُہستانی
The man of the desert of the mountains Alone can further the purposes of Nature[24].

---

[24] Muhammad. Iqbal, accessed Sep 2, 2017, https://www.iap.gov.pk/

Exercise

1. Celebrate spring to perform thanks.
2. Celebrate autumn to realize the end of life.
3. Celebrate grace of moon on the 14th of Lunar month by sharing knowledge about moon based on Quran, science and literature.
4. Watch nature before bed. You will have wonderful sleep and dream
5. Show children nature instead of cartoons. They will start to show peace.
6. Preach plants' rights, go for tree plantation, donate for water development schemes, e-g, dams or wells construction.
7. Preach animals' rights

The path to greatness consists of having a strong and genuine desire, a good purpose, and also having good company along the way--people who will help you endure as you walk through life for greatness isn't a one-time effort, it's a lifelong habit. Start bringing out the greatness in you and in others.

This moment you may have started to realize that you are immense inside and outside; Lets enjoy your greatness in following verses.

Iqbal says:

ستاروں سے آگے جہاں اور بھی ہیں ابھی عشق کے امتحاں اور بھی ہیں
There are yet more worlds beyond the Stars There are more examinations that love has yet to surpass
تہی، زندگی سے نہیں یہ فضائیں یہاں سینکڑوں کا روا ں اور بھی ہیں
This environment is not bereft of life There are thousand caravans that are yet to pass
قناعت نہ کر عالم رنگ و بو پر چمن اور بھی آشیاں اور بھی ہیں
Do not be satisfied by the colors and the smells of the present There are yet more undiscovered homes and gardens
اگر کھو گیا اک نشمین تو کیا غم مقا ما ت آہ و فغا ں اور بھی ہیں

Why do you grieve at having lost a loved one? There are many other places and reasons to cry
تو شاہیں ہے، پرواز ہے کام تیرا ترے سامنے آسماں اور بھی ہیں
You are a Falcon, and it is your purpose to soar Many open skies lie ahead in your path
اسی روز و شب میں الجھ کر نہ رہ جا کہ تیرے زمان و مکاں اور بھی ہیں
Do not get trapped by the day and the night Because you, have yet to discover more lands and spaces
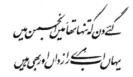
Gone are the days that I was lonely in society I now have more people to share my secrets[25].

Please rise to say:

May the kindness you spread to enhance your mutuality with the Creator, with the Humanity, and with the Nature keep returning to you many fold in this world and the world hereafter.

---

[25] Muhammad. Iqbal, accessed Sep 2, 2017, https://www.iap.gov.pk/

CHAPTER 7

THOUGHTFULLY INTELLIGENT INDIVIDUALS AND FORMAL MORAL DEVELOPMENT

"Caretaking of the Gardner turns the jungle into garden; and carelessness of the Gardner turns garden into jungle[1]." Quran says, "Allāh will exalt those of you who believe and those who are *given knowledge* to high degrees[2]."

Khizra's mentor 'Qareeb' **enlightens that in the class of kindness, there are no late comers, nor any back-benchers. He e**mphasizes that the dispersion of knowledge by the formal education system must be overarched by the 'Thoughtful Intelligence'. Thoughtful intelligence visions the eyes to observe and gives the courage[3] to understand befittingly suited to difficult times; and reveals compassion[4] for moral development. Therefore in 7th chapter I highlight the following:

    I.   Challenges to ormal moral development
    II. Opportunities for formal moral development
    III. Thoughtful corridors

---

[1] "Imam Ghazali Quotes," accessed July 2, 2018 https://www.google.com.pk/search?q=imam+ghazali+quotes
[2] Al-Quran, Al-Mujadila Ayat: 58-11
[3] Courage is the ability to do something that frightens one: bravery.
[4] Compassion is the ability to give and to forgive.

I. Challenges to formal moral development

The challenges invite us to engage in a contest to prove moral development. We have to participate in a competitive situation or fight to decide that moral development based on thoughtful intelligence is superior in terms of strength.

1. Normative statements in and around formal education arenas

The following statements have become increasingly normative. I call it challenge 'One', because such set of statements likens amoral trends.

-   Everybody has the right to do ---you should not be the judge of others? (General public)
-   What your (righteousness) effort will make the difference regarding the other powerful (thoughtless) trends? (General public)
-   So what if I start my class 20 minutes late? (Teacher)
-   So what if I do not teach about fairness[5], punctuality and patriotism? (Teacher)
-   So what if I arrive late in the class ----I am not short of attendance? (Student)
-   So what if I do not perform well in examination? (Student)

2. Grey vision and mission of education system

Grey means less focusing on moral development. Moral development exists in grey of the higher education vision. Only few systems are found making it a part of their mission. In the prevalent education system there is not a lot of active learning. The minds are not being challenged as the focus is to cover the curriculum at all costs. There is increasing criticism of standardized tests because they do not nurture the mind-sets to apply the formal knowledge to organize real life. The produced mind-sets 'DO NOT' understand and realize the impact of theirs' thoughts, words and actions on others' (individuals', groups', and nations') survival, dignity[6] and development in time (days, weeks, months or years) and space

---

[5] Fairness: Impartial and just treatment or behavior without favoritism or discrimination. Here fairness is to perform the role allocated in the system of humanity in general and specific as student and teacher.
[6] Al-Quran, Bani Israel, Ayat: 70 'And We have certainly honored the children of Adam'

(geographical land with or without human beings). The implications of such trends make the people to ask for training the mind-set.

Iqbal says:

مُدرسہ عقل کوآزاد تو کرتا ہے مگر   چھوڑ جاتا ہے خیالات کو بے ربط و نظام
The seat of learning gives the mind of pupils' scope.
But leave the thought of youth unlimited by thread of rope[7].

The state of the art lacks the nurturing of: Loyalty, Courage, Compassion, Humbleness, Integrity, Justice, responsibility. These items exist at competency level but not at performance level.

"If the mind-set is not reformed, no administrative, economic or constitutional reforms can save the country from the ever exacerbating inefficiency, corruption and malpractices. Governance involves not only administrative or managerial capacities but also the social, political, intellectual, cultural and moral capacities of a system in its entirety. And the best governance machinery is the one which harnesses all these capacities and directs their focused beam on the resolution of the problems that confront the nation. If, for example, intellectuals provide no fresh or creative ideas or if the culture of a nation is not generative of values of honesty, dedication, compassion and the like, the quality of governance will suffer, no matter how perfect are the institutional arrangements[8].

Iqbal says:

شکایت ہے مجھے یارب! خداوندانِ مکتب سے   سبق شاہین بچوں کو دے رہے ہیں خاکبازی کا
Slaves of custom are all the schools of old;
They teach the eagle to grovel in the dust[9]

As per our national practices our International recognition has overtaken us. And we seem to be overwhelmed by it. We do not know what tools to pick and which technology to apply to set the matter right. The crisis is not

---

[7] Muhammad. Iqbal, accessed Sep 2, 2017, https://www.iap.gov.pk/

[8] Jagmohan, Sumit. "Social and Cultural Capacities for Corruption-Free Governance", *India International Quarterly*, (Summer 2006)

[9] Muhammad. Iqbal, accessed Sep 2, 2017, https://www.iap.gov.pk/

structural as it is rooted in malpractices of the society. The guiding principle is: the Morals Education cannot be reared in the higher education without assessing the foremost thinking inclination of human beings. It is assumed that morals exist and persist because of thoughtfulness.

❖ The very strong question in society is: why our students/people do not show case moral values in their behavior?

❖ The other blazing question is how can we effectively promote moral values in students/people so that they adopt them?

Textual study alone does not necessarily translate into the moral conduct. To deal with the challenge of transforming the "knower" into the "doer; one (individuals, groups, nations) must follow the principles of moral development.

3. State of thoughtfulness literacy

Our survey regarding the prevalence of literacy of thoughtfulness brought us the following results. The magnitude about the manifestation of thoughtfulness is found at 35% as per results of Focused Delphi in the fifteen respondents (See Table 7.1) to reach consensus to define thoughtfulness.

Table 7. 1 Delphi Focused Sampling			
No of Experts	Domain	Cognate	Slot
5	Sciences and Technology	Sustainable Development	Decision making
5	Management	-	-
5	Social Sciences	-	-

Whereas the Exploratory Delphi results showcased 45% faculy and 85% students unfamiliar to the concept of thoughtfulness in the eight surveyed universities of Islamabad/Pakistan. 150 students from each of the eight universities in Islamabad were interviewed through the following guidelines to have the 'Conceptual Analysis of Thoughtfulness for Sustainable Decision Making' in the Pakistani Universities':

1. How you have encountered the word thoughtfulness in your *thinking*?
2. How you have encountered the word thoughtfulness in your *practice*?
3. How you *felt* when asked about the word thoughtfulness?
4. How you *feel* to opine about the word thoughtfulness?
5. How you *define* the word thoughtfulness?
6. How you define thoughtfulness *in general*?
7. How you define thoughtfulness *in specific*?

II. Opportunities for formal moral development

The set of circumstances makes it possible for us to employ comprehensive approach to promote moral development of students/ people. Here I propose principles of education, principles of leadership and principles of thoughtful intelligence to drive moral development. I highlight a research paper, 'Building Thoughtfulness ontology for Sustainable Decision Making[10].' I also show case seminar on 'Ethical Fitness' organized by the COMSATS University, Abbottabad/Pakistan as an example can be followed for moral development.

1. Principles of education[11]

"Aristotle created virtue ethics and taught that to become virtuous requires education in the virtues and practice in how to apply them. This dual emphasis on the insightful learning and behavior change remains with us in contemporary psychology[12]." The root of the word *education* is "to draw forth." Ideas are powerful when they motivate teachers and learners to cease doing business as usual and consider alternatives. For Arendt, teaching is a moral activity, an end in itself as well as a means to develop reflective and deliberate ethical behavior[13].

---

[10] Musarrat. Jabeen, "Building Thoughtfulness Ontology for sustainable decision making" *OIDA International Journal of Sustainable Development,* Vol 3 (Spring 2012): 35-40
[11] In ancient Greece, Socrates argued that education was about drawing out what was already within the student.
[12] "Stanford Encyclopedia of Philosophy: Aristotle's Ethics," accessed May 1, 2017, https://plato.stanford.edu/entries/aristotle-ethics
[13] Hannah. Arendt, *The Life of the Mind* (California: Harcourt Brace, 1981)

For Einstein, "Education is not the learning of facts, but the training of the mind to think[14]." To "do Good" is a systematic process of both thinking and doing[15]. "The aim of education is growth, both intellectual and moral[16]."

In morality, one cannot develop from the fear of punishment to guilt without developing the cognitive capacity to make moral self-judgments. Moral development includes; Teacher training, school counseling and parent education[17].

Moral: Moral clarity of values matters for Moral development.

2. Principles of leadership[18]

"I have full faith in my people that they will rise to every occasion worthy of past Islamic history, glory and traditions. My message to you all is of hope, courage and confidence[19]." "Let us mobilize all our resources in a systematic and organized way and tackle the grave issues that confront us with the grim determination and discipline worthy of a great nation[20]."

Iqbal says:

جہاں تازہ کی افکار تازہ سے ہے نمود   کہ سنگ وخشت سے ہوتے نہیں جہاں پیدا

New worlds derive their pomp from thoughts quite fresh and new
From stones and bricks a world was neither built nor grew[21].

---

[14] Albert Einstien "Einstein on Education" accessed March 3, 2018, https://theunityprocess. com/einstein-on-education

[15] Karen. Kitchener, *Foundations of Ethical Practice, Research, and Teaching in Psychology* (UK, Routledge: 2014)

[16] John. Deway, "Educationn and Growth." accessed April 3, 2018. https://genius.com/ John-dewey-education-as-growth-annotated

[17] Martin H. Ritchie, and Ronald L. Partin. "Parent Education and Consultation Activities of School Counselors" accessed Sep 2, 2017, https://eric.ed.gov/

[18] Leadership: The leaders of people, organization, or a country.

[19] Quaid-e-Azam's message to the nation on August 14, 1948, accessed Sep 2, 2017, https:// www.pips.gov.pk/

[20] Quaid-e-Azam message to the nation, EidulAdha, 24 October 1947, accessed Sep 2, 2017, https://www.pips.gov.pk/

[21] Muhammad. Iqbal, accessed Sep 2, 2017, https://www.iap.gov.pk/

3. Principles of thoughtful intelligence

The principles of thoughtful intelligence are as follows:

1. Observing self for self assessment and management. Prophet Muhammad (PBUH) says, "O my Lord! Increase me in knowledge."
2. Cleansing inside (Greater Jihad)
3. Realization of relationship with human and natural resources. Thoughtful intelligence counts the performance and not competence only.
4. Realization of future effects of decisions in time and space. Quran says, "Good and evil cannot be equal. [Prophet], repel evil with what is better and your enemy will become as close as an old and valued friend[22]."
5. Moral clarity; by an articulate human conception of moral justice. The student is supposed to incline to the respect and reverence for the Book of Quran. The objective is attainable by conducting "guided discussion."
6. An ultimate sense of action and not of inefficient action. Quran says, "[Prophet], call [people] to the way of your Lord with wisdom and good teaching. Argue with them with the most courteous way, for your Lord knows best who has strayed from his way and who is rightly guided[23]."
7. Thinking and realizing that where the actions are calculated; in the list of good deeds or in the list of bad deeds.

The route towards moral development depends on social connectivity referred to the interpersonal and intrapersonal values, virtues and behaviors caused by formal, informal and non formal education. While debating the moral development; the point of highlight is moral knowledge. The situation sets to harness the question: How to rear morals in the higher education? The moral disposition here is thoughtfulness as it is assumed that morals exist and persist because of the thoughtfulness. Particular concern is to establish the conceptual

---

[22] Al-Quran, Al- Fussilat, Ayat:34
[23] Al-Quran, Al-Nahl, Ayat:125

103

description and understanding of thoughtfulness among the faculty and students of higher education.

Research paper: 'Building Thoughtfulness ontology for Sustainable Decision Making.' The paper takes on board the concepts of thoughtfulness, and develops a Thoughtful Decision Support System. It emphasizes that Sustainable decision making depends on the level of thoughtfulness of decision makers. The conceptual basis of thoughtfulness involves three abilities. It requires: 1) an ultimate sense of action and not of inaction, 2) super-relationship with human and natural resources, and 3) awareness of future effects of decisions in time and space. Seven thoughtful Meta abilities are also chosen to establish the basis of this system. Thoughtfulness ontology adds a value of sustainability in decision making.

Sustainable decision making is parametric in positive impact on human and natural resources in the two scales of time and space. The decisions are found unsustainable mainly due to the thinking capacity of decision makers dependent on self, social, organizational, political and power Decision Support Systems (DSS). This paper proposes to flash thoughtfulness ontology to build a super DSS of thoughtfulness. Thoughtfulness promises a new vista of power. The paper evolves through the understanding of thoughtfulness.

Thoughtfulness is the capacity of showing understanding of what impact any act or word have on other person and refraining from it if one feels the impact will be negative; or making an effort to do it if the impact to be is positiveThoughtfulness consists of specific capacity whereby the decision maker longs for sustainability of his/her decision in time and space, whether his/her leadership status continues or not.

Ontology is useful in organizing knowledge, sharing knowledge, building consensus, and building knowledge based systems. Prima facie of thoughtfulness ontology concentrates on Decision Support Systems and Intelligence, to rim into Thoughtful Decision Support System, Thoughtful Intelligence and Thoughtful Meta Abilities.

Typically the top decisions are influenced by five DSSs named Self DSS, Social DSS, Organizational DSS, Political DSS and Power DSS (See Table 7. 2, Decision Support Systems). DSS analysis describes the position of a decision maker. Each DSS is viewed in terms of relations to sustainability with positive dynamics. The DSSs may contradict one another while being referred to a decision maker, they may also contradict while judged as what is done and what needs to be done. Thoughtfulness ontology may help to manage these contradictions.

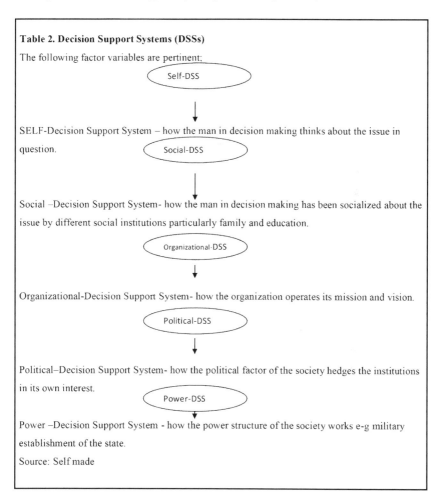

Table 2. Decision Support Systems (DSSs)

The following factor variables are pertinent;

Self-DSS

SELF-Decision Support System – how the man in decision making thinks about the issue in question.

Social-DSS

Social –Decision Support System- how the man in decision making has been socialized about the issue by different social institutions particularly family and education.

Organizational-DSS

Organizational-Decision Support System- how the organization operates its mission and vision.

Political-DSS

Political–Decision Support System- how the political factor of the society hedges the institutions in its own interest.

Power-DSS

Power –Decision Support System - how the power structure of the society works e-g military establishment of the state.

Source: Self made

Specific argument of the paper is that thoughtfulness can build consensus among the DSSs and efficiency in the hierarchy of DSSs; because thoughtfulness factors in decision making with sustainable intent and implications.

In this paper thoughtful intelligence consists of three basic abilities (See Figure 1, Conceptual Framework of Thoughtfulness) and seven

Meta abilities of Righteousness, Purposefulness, Understanding, Contemplation, Sincerity, Mindfulness and Nurturing.

The impact is that a thoughtful decision maker can make his/her presence felt in the future regardless of his existing status. A thoughtful decision maker is wise enough to know what to do. Knowing what to do? keeps one in the place of influence. A leader can be successful with the higher capacity of thoughtfulness.

By using thoughtfulness ontology suitable solutions can be reached to solve the uncertainty and reasoning problems in decision making.

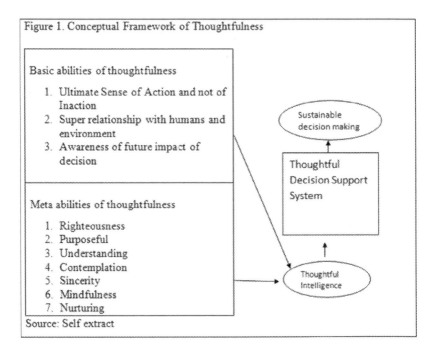

Figure 1. Conceptual Framework of Thoughtfulness

Thoughtfulness ontology may bring decision makers to realize the impact of their actions and inactions. Therefore, understanding thoughtfulness may be promoted through specific education programmed for managers, consultants, academia and political decision makers.

Thoughtfulness rejects normative practices of inaction, neglect of human and natural resources, and negative impact of decisions. Thoughtfulness is attainable but less likely to exist in normative planning and execution. Thoughtfulness is a conscious effort. It is found that mostly the decision makers from business, bureaucracy/military-civilian and politics are not equipped with thoughtfulness.

The concept developed in this study insinuates the paramount of thoughtfulness for sustainable decision making. Thoughtfulness is the ability to synthesize past, present and future of certain realms. Thoughtful decision makers think and then act. They critically establish value questions, fact questions. Thoughtful decision makers consolidate routinely attained knowledge about the multi realms they live in. Thoughtfulness is not only to use the available information but to realize more information resources---not only to allocate but to locate resources. Thoughtfulness DSS has become desirable due to globalization; wherein the monetary valuation of decisions is over whelming. Thoughtfulness uploads compassion and restrains to manage human and natural resources.

Seminar on 'Ethical Fitness': COMSATS Institute of Information Technology convened a dynamic national seminar/workshop entitled "Ethical Fitness: A Broader Perspective for Development" from 29th to 30th March 2013, in collaboration with the Higher Education Commission of Pakistan, Islamabad. The venue of the seminar/workshop was COMSATS Institute of Information Technology, Abbottabad. The proceedings of the seminar/conference touched upon the core issues of development from the perspectives of Ethical Fitness and highlighted the role which the higher education systems can play to address the identified relevant issues.

Ethical Fitness discusses the responses to different situations referred to different paradigms set by different mind-sets and maneuvers to manage the responses vis-à-vis the whole and component systems; as both of them impact each other.

The major objectives of the event were: (a) to give an overview of Ethical Fitness and its dynamics, (b) to create awareness among the audience about the Ethical Fitness and its impact on contemporary governance paradigms vis-à-vis development in Pakistan, (c) to assess the capacity of participants to further the cause of Ethical Fitness. Prior to the commencement of the seminar/workshop, the participants and the resource persons were requested that the direction of presentations/

discussions should be Pakistan-specific and ethics-centric. The following questions were attempted:

1. How to assess the loss of ethical values in contemporary socio-economic system of Pakistan?
2. How to establish ethical literacy in our educational and management institutions?
3. What can be the role of Higher Education institutions in designing Ethical Fitness programs and workshops?
4. How the Ethical Fitness discourse can be taken to policy making avenues?

A pre-seminar/workshop survey was conducted with a sample population of 300. The measured items were: punctuality, thanks giving, and prioritizing collectivism.

- 76% opined that they prefer to reach the event/meeting/workshop at prescribed time while 24% would reach after prescribed time.
- 05% expressed that they would like to win the project of 20 million worth in their own interest while 95% would like to win the same project in department's interest.
- 67% were of the view that they say thanks to their servants when he/she serves them a glass of water while 33% do not thank their servants on being served a glass of water by them.

The results were pertinent to benchmark the ethical capacity of the sample population because:

- The *people* who reach in time do not like to waste the resources of their own and of others and because of them the meetings become effective.
- The *people* who like to win project for their organization rather for themselves have more institutional kinship.
- The *people* who say thanks to their servants are closer to human kinship.
- The *people* who care for other's resources, organizations, and their servants have more ethical capacity and human kinship.

The results have certain limitations as the same trends may not be found in general public. The population was selected specific and inclined to Ethics knowhow.

The seminar/workshop was attended by 300 participants from various walks of life and different disciplines of the institutions. Four topics were chosen; 'Programming the Mind-set,' 'The Role of Faculty in Character Building,' 'Code of Ethics and Society,' 'The Ethics of Al-Ghazali: A Composite Ethics in Islam.' All these areas have saturated linkages with sustainable development of Pakistan. Efforts were made to identify the most important challenges and their Ethics supported solutions in realistic manner. The scholars delivered their technical presentations followed by question/answer sessions.

The first technical session was chaired by Dr. Pervez Ahmad Butt, the Founder Executive Director of COMSATS and former secretary Ministry of Science & Technology. He delivered his speech on 'Programming the Mind-set' inherently created ground for the next session. Dr. Mussarat Jabeen, Associate Professor, Department of Development Studies CIIT Abbottabad announced a surprise. It was rather a practical example of the Religious Ethics; she requested Brig. Nayer Firdous, Director of Studies, Pakistan Military Academy, Abbottabad, to cut the cake for the Easter celebration. She presented him a bouquet of flowers as well. 30th March was the Easter Day and Brig. Nayer Firdous belonged to the Christian religion.

Second technical session started with the song "Ya Rab dil-e-muslim ko wo zinda tamana dy" (O, Lord give aspiration to Muslim's heart). The dominating part of the session was the presentation by Dr. Syed Safdar Ali Shah, Director Academics National University of Sciences and Technology (NUST). He mapped out 'Ethics Education' and illuminated the role of faculty in character building of students. The presentation elaborated moral and academic role of educators in developing responsible 'graduates'. It emphasized the responsibility of faculty to develop and foster our young generation to make thoughtful decisions. Spring walk at the end of the session was organized. All the guests and participants enjoyed the spring walk and cherished by the spring spillovers in the premises of COMSAT, CIIT, Abbottabad. The appreciation of nature nourishes the ethical being.

The third technical session was the interesting one as it started with a mock session. Mock session highlighted twenty ethical issues regarding the faculty, parents and overall society's role in building the Ethics know how. Mock session was followed by a patriotic song "Wo din bhi ayega jab aesa hoga Pakistan". In this session the technical presentation was delivered by Prof. Dr. Farkhanda Aurangzeb, Manager Legislative Watch, Aurat Foundation Islamabad. Her topic was 'Code of Ethics and Society.' She focused on, If man was simply a machine then what room was left for morality? She said that we should avoid shortcuts. The younger generations should be taught to avoid shortcuts. Materialism takes away our sensibility and ability to judge. We should revitalize our knowledge sources. We should carry ourselves according to the code of ethics as we are judged by how we carry ourselves.

The fourth technical session started with a video clip which revealed that old age home is a popular concept now. We are becoming so materialistic that in the urge of more money we don't care for our sacred relations (parents). This video clip was followed by the technical presentation of Dr. Mumtaz Jaffari Advisor Faculty Development Academy COMSATS Islamabad, she enlightened the audience with the thoughts of Imam Al-Ghazali and personality development. The topic of her presentation was 'The Ethics of Al-Ghazali: A Composite Ethics in Islam'. She elaborated Ghazali's thought as, "Fear of God is pain in the heart and its burning because of the expectation of future adversities and the best fruit of this feeling is the opening of the soul's inner doors to a quiet hope." Mr. Saeed Akhtar, Advocate, President High Court Bar Association, Abbottabad delivered a notable note and he said today its time for team work to build our ethics and the common ethic around the globe is the ethic of humanity.

As a result of afore-mentioned sessions the following points emerged:

1. Pakistan's socio-economic fabric is being seriously eroded due to the crisis-level challenges related to Ethical values. These challenges are restricting Pakistan to come out of the abyss of poverty, ignorance, backwardness, extremism and law and order situation.

2. The seminar/workshop established that Ethical Fitness knowhow can be useful for producing quality education.
3. The knowhow of Ethical Fitness can be tailored and conducted like Political Ethics, Military Ethics, Bio Ethics, Intellectual Ethics as per requirements of the institutions and situations.
4. Institutional capacity building and human resource development for the identified Ethics knowhow integrated fields of interest should be given priority.
5. Educational reforms should be introduced to enrich the curricula and 'graduate profile' with Ethics knowhow component.
6. National policies, planning and strategies should aim to link to Ethics knowhow to resolve the identified crises.
7. Corruption was identified as the major retarding factor for Pakistan's progress. Ethical Fitness in public and private sector should be extensively practiced.

Government should make serious efforts to promote Ethics knowhow. The seminar/workshop proposed the establishment of a think tank as soon as possible to continue the cause of Ethical Fitness. Many young participants volunteered to help COMSATS for and specific aspects of the Ethical Fitness were taken up both in the presentations and in the application of social informatics. All the participants attended the event in its entirety.

After the seminar/workshop a feedback survey was carried out. The following narrative reflects the outcome. 85-89% participants came to know about the seminar/workshop through the organizers. It was the first time that they were able to attend the workshop on Ethical Fitness. They learnt the knowhow about honesty, respect for others and punctuality. The most effective speaker was Dr. Syed Safdar Ali Shah, Director Academics, NUST. The participants suggested to organize such workshops again as they would like to be the part of it. Take away of the workshop was:

• Comprehensive education of social issues as social innovation has a minute cost but magnificent effect.
• Development of ethical dispositions to develop social conscience

- Educational reforms to enrich the curricula and 'graduate profile' with Ethics knowhow component.

III. Thoughtful corridors

The period of time following the moment of thinking or writing this book; I contract the concepts and assets of thoughtful intelligence at agreed perception to deliver moral development at earliest possible.

I foresee the prevalence of moral development in the higher education and look forward to establish the thoughtful corridors among the societies of the people legislating and executing the policies for the business of humanity. Following are the stages:

Stage 1	Apply chapter 1-5
Stage 2	Apply chapter 6
Stage 3	Apply chapter 7

Thoughtful human life is the condition that distinguishes man from animals, and plants, including the capacity for growth, reproduction, functional activity, and *continual change* preceding death.

Iqbql says:

دل مردہ دل نہیں ہے ،اسی زندہ کردوبارہ   کہ یہی ہےامتوں کےمرض کہن کا چارہ
ترا بحر پرسکوں ہے، یہ سکوں ہے یا فسوں ہے؟   نہ نہنگ ہے،نہ طوفاں، نہ خرابی کنارہ!

A heart devoid of love is dead, Infuse fresh life in it again:
It is the only cure for folk who suffer from some chronic pain.
Your sea is full of calm and rest is it repose or magic art?
No sharks and storms disturb your sea,
intact its coast in every part![24]

Moral: Moral development is the need of present/future generations.

---

[24] Muhammad. Iqbal, accessed Sep 2, 2017, https://www.iap.gov.pk/

Exercise

Try this book

Please rise to say:

May we are able each moment to understand and realize the impact of our thoughts, words and actions on others' (individual, group, and nation) survival, dignity and development.

Printed in the United States
By Bookmasters